Progressing the Journey

*Lyrics and Liturgy
for a Conscious Church*

Susan Jones

Copyright © 2022 Susan Jones

All rights reserved.

Contact Susan at: jones.rs@xtra.co.nz

Churches, worship and small group leaders and choirs may freely copy and sing/use the hymns, songs, prayers and poems in this book.

This includes concerts and other events
for which admission is charged.

When doing so please credit:
Susan Jones: Progressing the Journey, 2022

If you want to include any of the material in this book in a commercial recording or publication, then please contact the publisher,
Philip Garside Publishing Ltd, by email, to arrange terms:
books@pgpl.co.nz

Paperback International edition:
ISBN 9781988572963

Also available

New Zealand Paperback edition: ISBN 9781988572925
Paperback print-on-demand USA: ISBN 9798419084803
ePub: ISBN 9781988572956
Kindle/Mobi: ISBN 9781988572949
PDF edition: ISBN 9781988572932

Sets of PowerPoint slides for the hymn lyrics in this book
are also available from the publisher.

Philip Garside Publishing Ltd
PO Box 17160
Wellington 6147
New Zealand

books@pgpl.co.nz — www.pgpl.co.nz

Cover photograph:
Sagrada Familia Church, Barcelona by Gaudi
Photo 168069553 / Church © Scott Biales | Dreamstime.com

Contents

Introduction 9
    Abbreviations used in the hymns section 10
Hymning the Journey — New words, familiar tunes 11
    A donkey walks his burden 12
    A safe stronghold we may seek still 13
    A wise poet wrote one day 14
    All people that on earth do hear 15
    Ancient words ring through the aeons 16
    And did those feet in former times 17
    As we meet 18
    Celebrate the Life we're given (1) 19
    Celebrate the Life we're given (2) 20
    Celebrate the life we're given (3) 21
    Each Lent we journey with a much-loved friend 22
    For all the saints (1) 23
    For all the saints (2) 24
    For all the saints (3) 25
    From ancient times the stories flowed 26
    Great is the glory of this newborn day 27
    Guide me now to climb the mountain 28
    I sing a song of the saints of God 29
    In our world we find delight 31
    It takes us effort 37
    Letters written to the churches 38
    Let us reach down deep inside us 39
    Now comes the bridegroom, the kingdom is near 40
    O when I see the awesome world 41
    On our life's journey 42
    Onward sacred pilgrims 43
    Our delight is in the broadness 44
    Rainbow God 45
    So many times 46
    The church needs a foundation 47
    The Treaty came here for the signing 48

The woman came 50
The year is ever turning 51
Through the crowds 52
To the wilderness so hostile 53
We bring thankful hearts 54
We give praise for the river's flow 55
We thank the men and women 56
What does it mean? 57
When I walk through bush so green 58
When we were young our God was huge 59
When life is filled with logic 60
Where can we learn greater loving? 61
Work for the night is here 62

Hymn Indexes 63
Topics and Themes 63
Bible References 64
The Church Year 64
Tunes 65

Wording our Worship — New words for new ideas 67

1 — Responsive Gatherings 68
Gathering for the First Sunday in Advent 68
Gathering for the Second Sunday in Advent 68
Gathering for the Fourth Sunday in Advent 69
Gathering for Christmas Eve 69
Gathering for the Third Sunday in Lent 69
Gathering for the Fourth Sunday in Lent 70
Gathering for the Fifth Sunday in Lent 70
Gathering for Palm Sunday 70
Gathering for After Easter Day 70
Gathering for Pentecost 71
Gathering to Consider Grace 71
Gathering to Consider Action 72
Gathering to Consider Spirituality 72
Gathering to Consider Faith 72
Gathering to Consider the Inner Journey 73

Gathering to Consider Life's Rhythm 73
Gathering for Creation Month 73
Gathering for Cosmos Sunday 74
Gathering for Reformers' Sunday 74
Gathering in an Inclusive Church 75
Gathering for Transgender Sunday 75
Gathering for Transgender Day of Remembrance 75
Gathering of a Welcoming Church 76
Gathering of an Inclusive Church 76
Gathering for Pride Sunday 76
Gathering for an Inclusive Service 77
Gathering for Pride Week 77
Gathering on Communion Sunday 77
Gathering on Communion Sunday 78
Gathering for Refugee Sunday 78
Gathering During Bible Month 78
Gathering During Bible Month 79

2 — Pairs of Responsive Gatherings and Affirmations 80

Gathering After a General Election 80
Affirmation for a New Era 80
Gathering for a Questioning People 81
Affirmation of Faith 81
Gathering During Pride Month 82
Affirmation for an Inclusive Church 82
Gathering for Palm Sunday 83
Affirmation of Faith for Palm Sunday 83
Gathering for Pentecost 84
Affirmation at Pentecost 84
Gathering on Disability Sunday 85
Affirmation for Disability Sunday 85
Gathering for a Series on Compassion 86
Affirmation for 1st Sunday in Series of Four on Compassion ..86
Gathering for the Second Compassion Sunday 87
Affirmation of Faith said as an Offering Prayer 87
Gathering on the Third Compassion Sunday 88

Affirmation..88
Gathering on the Fourth Compassion Sunday.........................89
Affirmation Of Faith said as an Offering Prayer.......................89
Gathering for Wilderness Sunday, Creation Month................90
Affirmation of Faith said as the Offering Prayer.....................91
Gathering for a Service Where We Consider Power after a General Assembly..92
Affirmation Of Faith 92
Gathering Prayer for Wilderness Sunday..................................93
Confession 93
Prayer for Ourselves and Others for Wilderness Sunday.........94

3 — Creeds...95
Creed for an Easter People...95
Creed about Love...96
Creed from South Canterbury, New Zealand 97

4 — Affirmations..98
Affirmation for Advent Sunday..98
Affirmation for the Second Sunday in Advent 99
Affirmation of Prophets for the Third Sunday in Advent...... 100
Affirmation and Recognition of Faith Found in Epiphany.... 101
Affirmation of Wilderness for the First Sunday in Lent......... 102
Affirmation Under a Fig Tree for the Third Sunday In Lent . 103
Affirming the Waste of Perfume on the Fifth Sunday of Lent 104
Affirmation of Faith for Easter... 105
An Easter Affirmation on Being Human.................................. 106
An Anzac Affirmation of the Work of Peacemaking.............. 107
An Affirmation and Lament for Relationship on Trinity Sunday.. 108
Affirmation of the Feminine 109
Affirmation of the Word for Bible Month................................ 110
A Wondering Affirmation 111
An Affirmation which Celebrates a Different Way................. 112
An Affirmation of Water at a Baptism 113
Affirmation of Faith on the Fault line....................................... 114
Affirmation of Faithful Inclusion 115

Affirmation of Faith on an Anniversary 116
Affirmation of Compassion 117
Affirmation of Faith for a Learning Church 118
Celebration of Faith 119

5 — Pairs of Responsive Gatherings and Blessings 120
Easter Day 120
    Gathering 120
    Blessing 120
    Gathering 121
    Blessing 121
A Musical Service 122
    Gathering 122
    Blessing 122
    Gathering 123
    Blessing 123
    Gathering 124
    Blessing 124
Creation Month 125
    Gathering For Planet Sunday 125
    Blessing 125
After The Christchurch Massacre, March 2019 126
    Gathering 126
    Blessing 126

6 — Prayers 127
Lord's Prayer 127
Offering Prayer 128
Prayer of Adoration and Confession 128

7 — Lament and Litany 129
Thanksgiving and Lament 129
Litany of Thanksgiving 130

8 — Communion Liturgies 132
Great Prayer of Thanksgiving for the Season of Creation 132
Great Prayer of Thanksgiving for Peace and Justice 133
Communion Liturgy from the South Pacific 135
Great Thanksgiving for World Communion Sunday 137

9 — Responsive Blessings 138
Blessing on Matariki 138
Blessing for Wilderness Sunday 138
Blessing for Those Who Journey 138
Blessing for the Third Sunday in Advent 139
Blessing for the Fourth Sunday in Advent 139

10 — Poems 140
Advent 140
    The Door 140
    Midnight 141
Christmas 142
    Morning After the Night Before 142
Lent 143
    Brought to Tears 143
    There's not much beautiful about being broken 144
Easter 146
    Unseasonable journey 146
    Today 149
Pentecost 150
    Spirit Wind 150
    Aotearoa Pentecost 151
    A 'Silent' Pentecost 152

11 — Reflections from a New Perspective 153
Truth and Factuality: Babies and Stardust
– a Reflection for Christmas Day on Luke 2 153
The Storm on the Lake – Mark 4:35-41 155
Different kinds of waste – Luke 15:11-32 156

Recent & forthcoming books by Susan Jones
from Philip Garside Publishing Ltd **158**

Introduction

Welcome to new ways of speaking about and singing the journey.

This book comes out of 25 years of worship. As I led congregations over those years, I discovered that available hymns and liturgy no longer fitted the new ideas we now wish to reflect upon.

One discovery was particularly stark. I eagerly embraced the Season of Creation lectionary format. Looking for hymns to sing the first Season, I turned to Creation sections of conventional hymnbooks. Imagine my dismay. All their Creation hymns were about harvest – what we could get from the earth rather than what we could give to the earth. It was a symbolic moment. I realised that religion has contributed to the environmental fragility of our world. I found no hymns in conventional hymnbooks which were pro-environmental care. The New Zealand Hymnbook Trust has since redressed this imbalance.

Our understanding of the cosmos is no longer limited to the sun, moon, and stars. Black holes and bosons, quarks and dark matter are part of our everyday language. Communication methods now include Twitter, and texting. Saints may ride skateboards or study in science labs, not just be shepherdesses on the green.

The hymns and liturgies in this book reflect elements of our New Zealand landscape; tussocks, scree slopes, braided rivers, volcanoes and the Aurora Australis. Now, in the right season, we can sing our own metaphors.

Few conventional hymns name the reality of being LGBTQI. Rainbow communities need to be named and celebrated, just like other communities in our land.

I have found that people want to keep singing familiar tunes. We don't, however, want to cringe at the words or have to madly translate them on the fly all the time. I hope you enjoy the blend of old tunes and new words.

Our liturgies need updating too. New words are needed to describe the re-enchanted spiritual journey. Few liturgies express the realities of Disability Sunday and Pride Week, or offer a Communion liturgy with ideas about God and Jesus other than atonement theology. I want to name different types of power, the beauty of the cosmos and describe how to fit compassion more fully into our lives.

The lyrics and liturgy in this book can be used in worship, both conventional and alternative.

Please acknowledge the source – *Susan Jones: Progressing the Journey, 2022* – when using this material in PowerPoint slides, printed orders of service or when posting it online.

My thanks especially to John Hargreaves (Timaru) and Peter Franklin, (Wellington), two organists who inspired me to write well. Also thank you, Vivien Chiu, your beautiful music for the Creation hymn also was an inspiration. It is a bonus having a publisher keen on music – thank you Philip.

If some lyrics and words go too far for you, (in theology, or in sexual orientation and identity) then, rather than adapt them, please do not use them until you are more comfortable with the ideas they express. If you need geographical adjustments for another hemisphere, please make them. We in the southern hemisphere know it's annoying to have to sing/say words from the other half of the world!

Mostly, I hope you will enjoy the chance to sing and speak in our own vernacular, to be at home where we live, to name the realities of 21st century life.

May this book help your journeys to always be progressing towards a more loving and compassionate world.

Susan Jones
www.jonessmblog.wordpress.com
February 2022

Abbreviations used in the hymns section

AA	*Alleluia Aotearoa*
BHB	*Baptist Hymn Book (1962)*
CH4	*Church Hymnary 4th edition*
FFS	*Faith Forever Singing*
HTC	*Hymns for Today's Church 2nd edition*
TIS	*Together in Song*
WOV	*With One Voice*

Hymning the Journey — New words, familiar tunes

A donkey walks his burden
Carol commissioned by Christian World Service 2018

1. A donkey walks his burden onward
   telling us that Advent's on the way.
   Bearing Mary, bearing Jesus,
   under his load, the donkey sways.
   We rejoice to see this journey,
   for it offers hope and joy.
   We rejoice to hear this story,
   for it means much more than "It's a Boy!"

2. Worldwide, donkeys bear great burdens
   From ancient Israel to Haiti.
   Bearing people, bearing cargo,
   working through the day on tired feet.
   They are transport for the poor
   often being asked for more.
   They are key to family business,
   they are animals worth giving for.

3. When the baby Jesus grew, he
   taught compassion was the way.
   He believed we should give water,
   feed the hungry, love each day.
   Dignity is paramount, for
   humankind and donkeys too.
   Every Advent, let's remember
   all those who are carrying burdens new.

Tune: Nos Galan
(Deck the Halls with Boughs of Holly)

Susan Jones

A safe stronghold we may seek still
A hymn for a 21st century Reformation

1. A safe stronghold we may seek still,
   secure and safe, a loving embrace.
   We look in different places, will
   career and fam'ly take God's place?
   We seek a grounded life,
   an anchor in the strife,
   a centre point of calm,
   hurts healed by holy balm;
   Warm welcome at the gate to home.

2. We unwrap layers from ourselves,
   the baggage, stress and woundings,
   to find the Self which lives within,
   where we can make deep soundings.
   We find there kindness, light,
   creative, sweet delight,
   the heart which helps us thrive,
   where routine comes alive,
   a stronghold sure, in our deepest soul.

3. The energy we draw from there,
   lights beacons which flame living hope,
   and fuels for all a warm, bright care
   pushing back dark, so all can cope.
   Then justice flows free too,
   compassion flowers anew,
   for everyone is free,
   loved always, you and me,
   our common wealth undisputed.

Tune: Ein' Feste Burg
(WOV 8)

A wise poet wrote one day
A hymn about asking questions

1. A wise poet wrote one day,
   answers do not show the way.
   He said questions stretch us, so
   living questions help us grow.

2. Some enquiries are quite quick,
   "Where's my bag?" or "What's your pick?"
   Other queries take more time,
   "How did earth form?" "What makes rhyme?"

3. Questions exercise our brains,
   introduce us to the famed
   people who invent and make,
   those who write, compose, and paint.

4. God's a topic to research;
   "Is God present outside church?"
   "When I feel, do I 'feel' God?"
   "Is God a noun, or verb, or 'odd'?"

5. There's no question Love is good,
   brightening up the neighbourhood.
   Love can be both firm and kind,
   welcomes all, leaves none behind.

6. Questions widen up our world,
   stretch our faith, our hearts unfurl.
   They help us to show Love more,
   and make equal rich and poor.

Tune: Gentle Jesus
(WOV 545)

All people that on earth do hear

A hymn for the 175th anniversary of St Andrew's on The Terrace

1. All people that on earth do hear,
   this parish has for all these years,
   known all the numinous delight
   of faithful Love, transforming Light.

2. Scots brought their faith to Petone Beach,
   and celebrated Love's wide reach.
   From 1840, worship's been
   our way to ground Christ in our scene.

3. For many here found their first faith,
   which morphs as they new meanings make.
   God has been constant and aloof,
   weaving in us both warp and woof.

4. O'er all our worship and our moods,
   Wairua Tapu[1] always broods,
   forgiving ill, willing to heal,
   hosting at each communion meal.

5. For all who've gathered here to pray,
   for worshippers, and music played,
   for liturgy and Word preached true,
   we thank those faithful, brave first few.
   Amen.

Tune: Old 100th
(WOV 10)

This hymn was written specifically for St Andrew's on The Terrace, Wellington, New Zealand. By omitting verse 2 the hymn may be relevant in other settings.

---

[1] *Wairua Tapu* is Māori for Holy Spirit. It could be replaced by the words "the Holy Spirit" or "the loving Spirit"

Ancient words ring through the aeons
A hymn to celebrate prophets

1. Ancient words ring through the aeons,
   urging, chiding, giving praise.
   Prophets all, both men and women,
   led the people through life's maze.
   They were those who lived the message
   of the true life, spirit-filled.
   They were leaders through life's passage,
   leading with a courageous will.

2. Living simply, prophets focus
   on the truth and how to live;
   They read well the hearts of people,
   speaking from the Word, they give
   warnings, guidelines for true living,
   bravely they speak truth to power.
   They see through pretence and posture,
   they see when our leaders cower.

3. Knowing truth requires right action,
   speaking out, and staying true,
   to the prophets' ancient notions,
   knowing me and knowing you.
   May we now, like them, envision
   worlds where real compassion reigns,
   where love shows its many faces,
   where true justice is sustained.

Tune: Hyfrydol
(WOV 173)

And did those feet in former times

A hymn about Jesus walking Aotearoa NZ

1. And did those feet in former times,
   walk upon scree and tussock brown?
   And did the man, Jesus the Christ,
   cross mountains high and rolling downs?
   And did he know the morning mist?
   And did he know the harbour's sheen?
   And did he love the cityscape,
   its terraced streets, the urban scene?

2. And does he still walk this our land,
   talking and laughing with us yet?
   And does he know that stab of need,
   when neighbours snub, and worse, neglect?
   And is he there when wine is poured?
   And is he there when bread's prepared?
   And does he smile when good is done?
   And does he weep when conflict's flared?

3. And does he still build up his church,
   here in the context of our land?
   And does he look for living stones,
   and are we ready to his hand?
   To be transformed by Spirit's power,
   may we be opened up to grace.
   Till we are builded here, fresh, anew,
   in this homeland, this pleasant place.

4. Be with us Christ, as we step out,
   come with us on our lifelong quest.
   Be our true guide, on our right hand,
   be with us, walking and at rest.
   So we will know life to the full,
   be there to see us through the night.
   For we would be your followers,
   pursue your Way with all our might.

Tune: Jerusalem
(CH4 106)

As we meet

Interfaith Hymn for after Communion

1. As we meet memories bring to mind all those
   Who met us here in days now long ago;
   Offered the Bread, they gratefully received,
   sipped at the Cup, marvelled at Love's bright show.

2. Though not at table with us, there are others,
   who feast right now on sacredness and truth,
   who savour love, divine, peaceful and true;
   we honour pathways trod by sister faiths.

3. This table round has room for all the world;
   It is not ours, our church's, but for all.
   We feast together, this we fam'ly call,
   Joined now by love, and kin for good or ill.

4. As we move out, the world calls to our hearts;
   Many are grieving, deep in dark despair;
   Compassion moves within, eyes start to smart,
   May we be brave and show Love's always near.

Tune: Langran
(CH4 664 (a), HTC 406)

Celebrate the Life we're given (1)
A hymn for a baptism

1. Celebrate the Life we're given,
   grace on grace, where love abounds.
   Celebrate the world around us,
   blue and green, where birdsong sounds.
   Celebrate sun's rise and setting,
   'cross the harbour, over hills.
   Everything reflects its making,
   beauty, love, joy; each heart fills.

2. Celebrate the life born to us
   through a baby's welcome birth.
   Celebrate the new explosion
   of love's joy, delight and mirth.
   We see promise, hope and meaning
   in this life, begun this way.
   May this child, though little-seeming,
   add love to our world each day.

3. We choose to live lives of meaning,
   even when the sky turns grey.
   We choose to continue journeying,
   cis and trans, bi, straight and gay.
   We choose wrestling with doubt or danger,
   trials may shadow, haunt our way.
   But we know that we're companioned,
   Love walks with us, every day.

Tune: Austria
(WOV 577)

Celebrate the Life we're given (2)

A hymn to celebrate Pride Week

1. Celebrate the Life we're given,
   grace on grace, where love abounds.
   Celebrate the world around us,
   blue and green, where birdsong sounds.
   Celebrate sun's rise and setting,
   'cross the harbour, over hills.
   Everything reflects its making,
   beauty, love, joy; each heart fills.

2. We choose to live lives of meaning,
   even when the sky turns grey.
   We choose to continue journeying,
   cis and trans, bi, straight and gay.
   We choose wrestling doubt or danger,
   trials may shadow, haunt our way.
   But we know that we're companioned,
   love walks with us, every day.

3. Just as rainbows shine through rainfall,
   Love refracts our darkest day.
   We are birthed from one great light Source,
   red, through green, to purple's ray.
   Just as colour comes from one energy,
   we're made in one image, see!
   All one family, all one Spirit,
   all are loved, including me.

Tune: Austria
(WOV 577)

Celebrate the life we're given (3)
Hymn to celebrate life after a tragedy

1. Celebrate the Life we're given,
   grace on grace, where love abounds.
   Celebrate the world around us,
   blue and green, where birdsong sounds.
   Celebrate sun's rise and setting,
   'cross the harbour, over hills.
   Everything reflects true beauty,
   Love, Joy, Spirit; each heart fills.

2. We choose to live lives of meaning,
   even when the sky turns grey.
   We choose to continue journeying,
   Taking brave steps, straight, bi, gay.
   We choose wrestling with doubt or danger,
   Trials which shade and haunt our way.
   Every moment we're companioned,
   Love walks with us, every day.

3. We companion others grieving
   for their children, cruelly killed.
   Hearts reach out in love and comfort
   to homes where the laughter's stilled.
   May the love of friend and neighbour
   soothe the heart, and nerve the soul;
   May our world find good solutions,
   understanding self our goal.

4. Change takes us in new directions,
   altering our daily view.
   Change of style and life and custom,
   changing me and changing you.
   Still divine Love remains constant,
   though we find more that is true.
   Each day opens fresh horizons,
   breaks out truth that's overdue.

Tune: Austria
(WOV 577)

Each Lent we journey with a much-loved friend
A hymn for a Lenten communion

1. Each Lent we journey with a much-loved friend,
   the days are long, the path beneath us wends
   up hill and down, to valleys deep and frightening
   where night falls quickly, courage must be found.
   The path unfolds, we walk with our companion,
   who knows the way, the place to where we're bound.

2. Here on this path, we need someone to feed us
   the living bread, which nourishes our soul,
   to give us wine which slakes our thirst and buoys us,
   for each new day some trial may unfold.
   At this broad table, gathered round together,
   we all are fed and blessed and so made bold.

3. This table round allows each one to gather,
   there are no corners where we might get lost.
   Each one is equal, each one loved, accepted;
   For each the cup, the space, the love, the host.
   Gen'rous the sharing, all get more than crumbs;
   In all we're given, we gain love the most.

Tune: Finlandia
(WOV 48)

Can be used any communion Sunday by replacing
'Each Lent' by 'this day' or 'Today'

For all the saints (1)

Hymn for Transgender Day of Remembrance

1. For all the saints of every age and day,
   who bravely seek to follow Jesus' way,
   sharing Good News by what they do and say:
   Alleluia! Alleluia!

2. For those who struggle much with who they are,
   listening to feelings which with bodies jar,
   who seek and ask and travel near and far:
   Alleluia! Alleluia!

3. For those who understood, as feelings grew,
   the need to live within a body true,
   and all that's needed to change and renew:
   Alleluia, Alleluia

4. For Jesus, who exploded people's view,
   of who were 'out' or 'in' the chosen few,
   who died for freedom out of love for you:
   Alleluia, Alleluia.

5. And so we meet to celebrate the right,
   to be yourself by day and every night,
   in hope Love's flame will always burn for right:
   Alleluia! Alleluia!

Tune: Sine Nomine
(WOV 384)

For all the saints (2)

A hymn for questioners

1. For all the saints of every age and day,
   who bravely seek to follow the right way,
   sharing Good News by what they do and say:
   Alleluia! Alleluia!

2. For those who wrestle with ideas and faith;
   listen, discuss, sense of it all to make;
   risking exclusion, dislocation, hate:
   Alleluia! Alleluia!

3. For those who knew a better way to be,
   who stood and argued, so that all could see
   that each are needed for equality:
   Alleluia, Alleluia

4. For Jesus who exploded people's view,
   of who was 'out' or 'in' the chosen few,
   who died for freedom out of love for you:
   Alleluia, Alleluia.

5. And so we meet to celebrate the brave
   standing for good, who with compassion, gave
   their lives for truth, a Better Way to pave:
   Alleluia! Alleluia!

Tune: Sine Nomine
(WOV 384)

For all the saints (3)

Hymn for Mothers' Day

1. For all the saints of every age and day,
   who bravely seek to follow Jesus' way,
   sharing Good News by what they do and say:
   Alleluia! Alleluia!

2. For hidden saints, who kept home fires alight,
   nurturing faith through even darkest night,
   that in our day Love's hope may still burn bright:
   Alleluia! Alleluia!

3. For those we know, whose given task was care,
   who may have had to struggle to be fair,
   and through their lives, faith, healing, love to share:
   Alleluia! Alleluia!

4. For sisters, wives, aunts, nieces, mothers too,
   grandmothers, girlfriends, partners old and new,
   midwives of faith, still bringing in the true:
   Alleluia, alleluia.

5. For women who work in the public place;
   dealing in law, in business, all at pace,
   drivers and builders, carving out new space:
   Alleluia, alleluia

6. For women's work for justice and for peace,
   for those who suffer and need Love's release,
   for all our children, may war someday cease:
   Alleluia! Alleluia!

Tune: Sine Nomine
(WOV 384)

From ancient times the stories flowed

A hymn about healing

1. From ancient times the stories flowed
   From the Storyteller's heart;
   Sons and servants, seeds that grow,
   Jesus taught with loving heart.

   By words and actions, clear and bright,
   He brought life and love and light.

2. In the temple Jesus taught
   on the Sabbath calm and still.
   People listening, as they thought,
   heard his words of truth and skill.

   By words and actions, clear and bright,
   He brought life and love and light.

3. Then he saw a crooked back
   needing healing, love and more.
   He supplied it, earning flak
   from those who revered the law.

   By his actions, clear and bright,
   Transformed was her crippled life.

4. We the story tellers now,
   spelling out what's just and right.
   Should the Law to people bow?
   Or should Law insist it's right?

   By word, by actions, left and right,
   To our world bring love and light.

Tune: Lucerna Laudoniae
(WOV 77)

Great is the glory of this newborn day
A hymn for Easter Day

1. Great is the glory of this newborn day,
   Sunrise gilds the harbour, sparkles on the waves,
   Children shout with wonder, old men greet the sun,
   All refreshed, transformed by the Creating One.

   Great is the glory of this newborn day,
   Life is full, abundant, opening up the way!

2. Great is the glory of this brand-new day,
   Life is bright when Spirit shows us all the Way.
   Kowhai, 'hutukawa bask in Love's bright rays,
   Earth and sky and sea combine in fervent praise.

   Great is the glory of this newborn day,
   Life is full, abundant, opening up the way!

3. Sunshine now warms us from the chill of night,
   Healed to grow and flourish, graced to love, not fight.
   People from the margins find space in the sun.
   Women, men, non-binary, find old ways are done.

   Great is the glory of this newborn day,
   Life is full, abundant, opening up the way!

4. Life's not just only sunshine everyday.
   Sometimes darkened shadows with light interplay.
   Wholeness is the goal we juggle in our time,
   Real people, not just plaster saints, suit Jesus fine!

   Great is the glory of this newborn day,
   Life is full, abundant, opening up the way!

Tune: Maccabaeus
(WOV 303)

Guide me now to climb the mountain

Journeying seen in the Bible

1. Guide me now to climb the mountain,
   led by ancient sages old;
   Matriarchs, and prophets tell us
   how to journey, to be bold;
   Ancient writers, led by Spirit,
   found their way and show us ours,
   found their way and show us ours.

2. Though their times were then, not now,
   human issues are the same;
   Missionaries, writers all found
   life was more than Empire's fame;
   They stood strong with inner courage,
   they proclaimed a journey true,
   they proclaimed a journey true.

3. Scripture's words, obscure and puzzling
   to our eyes, yet show the way;
   Law and hist'ry, prophets, authors,
   tell the truth found in their day;
   Sacred was their constant calling,
   we need follow them today,
   we need follow them today

Tune: Cwm Rhondda
(WOV 478)

I sing a song of the saints of God

1. I sing a song of the saints of God;
   all those who live right now.
   They're tall and short and in between,
   all saints, please take a bow!
   And one is a skateboarder, one is a geek,
   And some play basketball every week.
   And being a saint is what they all seek,
   and I want to be one too.

2. I sing a song of the saints of God,
   'specially when they are girls.
   They wear pigtails, hang by fingertips,
   their life is just a whirl!
   You can meet them in studios, classrooms or labs,
   You can message, or text or just chill being fab.
   To be the best girl-saint they do seek,
   and I want to be one too.

3. I sing a song of the saints of God,
   'specially when they are boys.
   They might like cars or dance like stars,
   being active they enjoy.
   You can see them in libraries and sportsfields and such.
   Maybe playing music or playing touch.
   To be the best boy-saint they do seek,
   and I want to be one too.

4. I sing a song of the saints of God,
   'specially when they are free,
   to act like a girl or be like a boy,
   or sometimes in between.
   You can see them in theatre or gym or in class,
   their pronoun is 'they' and they're quite a blast.
   Non-binary sainthood is what they seek
   and I just might be one too.

5. I like to meet all the saints at church,
   that's where a lot are found.
   They're boys and girls, they're young or old,
   and they're great to be around.
   It's trying to do what Jesus would
   that makes them fun, and makes them good,
   for every saint tries to do what they should,
   and I want to be one too.

Tune: Grand Isle
(BHB 259, WOV 551)

In our world we find delight
Hymn for the Season of Creation

1. In our world we find delight,
   For creation, day and night,
   Brings us solace, joy;
   Spirit grows, refreshes, gleams,
   as the earth fuels richer dreams
   just by being here;
   May this beauty never end,
   May this solace always be here,
   May the human race take notice
   And show divine compassion.

2. Maui dolphin skims the waves,
   Gray and sleek, graceful at play,
   Aotearoa's child;
   Paua clings beneath the tide,
   Hiding beauty deep inside,
   Aotearoa's jewel;
   May this beauty never end,
   May this blueness always be here,
   May the human race take notice
   And show divine compassion.

3. Dark to light flies on the moth,
   Mottled, marked, like linen cloth,
   Only found right here;
   Hiding in the darkest nest,
   Kiwi like the night the best,
   Only found right here;
   May this beauty never end,
   May this brownness always be here,
   May the human race take notice
   And show divine compassion.

4. Kauri reaches to the light,
   Strong and powerful, full of might,
   Giant of the trees;
   Delicate, the orchid climbs,
   Over branches, green moss-lined,
   Swaying in the breeze;
   May this beauty never end,
   May this greenness always be here,
   May the human race take notice
   And show divine compassion.

5. Tui, iridescent coat,
   Singing from a trembling throat
   Crowns New Zealand's bush;
   Kereru with mighty wings,
   Blue and purple plumage brings
   To New Zealand's bush;
   May this beauty never end,
   May this iridescence stay here,
   May the human race take notice
   And show divine compassion.

6. Storm brings dark clouds, water falls,
   Lightning's crash astounds us all
   As the front rolls in;
   Rain that lashes window panes
   Brings new life to parched farmland
   Rehydrating fields;
   May this beauty never end
   May this rain continue watering
   May the human race take notice
   And show divine compassion.

7. Mountains march to distant heights
   Wilderness tests all our might
   Where the tussocks blow;
   Windswept tors define the land,
   Desert plateaus, mountains stand,
   Old eruptions' scars;
   May this beauty never end,
   May this rock and earth remain here,
   May the human race take notice
   And show divine compassion.

8. Looking into starry skies,
   Galaxies defeat our eyes,
   Distant stardust glows;
   Spinning planets circle suns,
   Stars are born, supernovae stun,
   Cosmos is our 'hood;
   May this beauty never end,
   May this universe remain here,
   May the human race take notice
   And show divine compassion.

9. Water trickles, rushes, spouts,
   Deep calm lakes drain to river mouth,
   Power wrested from snow;
   Humans, animals and plants
   need hydration, need the chance
   to refresh and grow;
   May this beauty never end,
   May this water last for everyone,
   May the human race take notice
   And show divine compassion.

10. Planet Earth spins like a jewel.
    Let us care and not be cruel
    To this treasured gem;
    This blue teardrop hanging here,
    Children's' children need a share.
    We owe this to them;
    May this planet always flourish,
    May its children still inherit,
    May we help this star to shine bright
    Show Earth divine compassion.

11. Let's endorse humanity,
    Part of Earth's full family,
    All made welcome here;
    Many genders, races, tribes,
    Personalities that jibe,
    All are welcome here;
    May all people feel accepted,
    Nations show true understanding,
    May all humans love each other
    And show divine compassion.

12. Skies stretch over all our lives,
    Prides of lion to bees in hives,
    All bask in the sun;
    Clouds race through as gale winds blow,
    Cirrus high and stratus low,
    Skies are bright or glum;
    May the air be always fragrant,
    And its clarity untainted;
    May the human race take notice
    And show divine compassion.

13. Land provides our standing place,
    hills through which the rivers trace,
    give us space to be;
    Ground which holds us, gives us base,
    needs our care, through all our days
    so it will survive;
    May this place continue standing,
    May this earth continue holding,
    May our feet be ever grounded
    Held in divine compassion.

14. It's a mystery who made this –
    evolution, hand-made care –
    multiple ideas.
    But it's not a mystery who
    Needs to care for green and blue –
    We have all been charged.
    To make sure this never ends,
    That this beauty does remain here,
    That the human race takes notice
    And shows divine compassion.

Tune: In our world we find delight

This hymn is intended to be sung in a 'kitset' fashion during the Season of Creation in the month of September. (See the *Revised Common Lectionary*.) See also: https://seasonofcreation.com/

The first and last verses are always to be sung. In between, insert, from the remaining verses, as many verses as you wish to match the week's Creation theme. This music and these words can be freely reproduced for use in worship.

The music on the following pages is copyright Vivien Chiu (2016) and is used with her permission.

In our world we find delight

Words: Susan Jones
Music: Vivien Chiu

Words © 2017-18 Susan Jones. Music © 2016 Vivien Chiu
All Rights Reserved

It takes us effort

A hymn about orthopraxis and offering

1. It takes us effort to give things away;
   Our money, or goods, or our time, many ways.
   We know we are charged with relieving the poor
   and charity always demands of us more.

2. It takes great effort to advocate true,
   for those who need systems to be well renewed;
   through marches, submissions, we seek human rights,
   but are distant from those for whom we might fight.

3. It takes much more effort to welcome right in
   the different, or 'other', those who never win;
   to make space as equals, and share goods with all
   requires us to relegate our needs to the call.

4. It takes most effort to incarnate the Christ,
   to work contr'y to this world's great power and might;
   to be 'with' the other not only do 'for',
   to be equal humans, equal right to the core.

Tune: Slane
(WOV 445)

Letters written to the churches

The epistles from the point of view of the Reformation

1. Letters written to the churches,
   give our earliest glimpses how
   Jesus seemed to his generation,
   who he was, both then and now;
   They debated his role and stature,
   seeking how they should react;
   How to meet and how to worship,
   sorting anecdotes from the facts.

2. Paul with others travelled the circuit,
   calming, urging, making things plain;
   Nurt'ring those who followed Jesus,
   linking all groups into the main;
   Creed and doctrine so developed,
   rites and rituals grew to be,
   customs, practice, all were fashioned
   through words penned by such as he.

3. Writers then used ink and parchment,
   texting now is short and sharp;
   Twitter, in the heat of the moment,
   limits thought, can exclude heart;
   How will we in our generation,
   let our wisdom have good space,
   put our time to thinking through issues,
   deal with others in love and grace?

4. Thanks be giv'n to those before us,
   who wrote words both living and true,
   spent hard time in prison and travel
   to ensure good news got through;
   Thanks to those who carried those letters,
   for the danger and risks they took,
   all combining to remind us
   Love shines forth, from this sacred book.

Tune: Blaenwern
(WOV 165 (ii))

Let us reach down deep inside us
A hymn about finding the Self within

1. Let us reach down deep inside us,
   to the place where quiet reigns;
   Find the Self who lives inside us,
   knows our joy and knows our pains:
   Let our ego stand aside there,
   shadow sharing space with light.
   Let our inner selves rejoice at how
   Love shines in darkest night.

2. Wind and fire and earthquake pass,
   but Spirit is not found in them;
   Still, small voice is hardly heard,
   but brings Love which does not condemn.
   In lives buffeted by windstorms,
   rocked by quakes, and scorched by fire,
   stillness brings surprising solace
   as we find there, hearts' desire.

3. Sacred calm means minds can settle,
   hearts grow quiet, souls grow still;
   Busy thinking slows its rhythm,
   gives compassion chance to fill.
   Even long-forgotten scars heal
   as new balm brings a new way;
   Every space, and every crevice
   fills, as Love arrives to stay.

Tune: Gaelic Traditional Melody
Arranged by John Bell.
(FFS 10 (i))

Now comes the bridegroom, the kingdom is near

A hymn about growing consciousness

1. Now comes the bridegroom, the kingdom is near,
   for deep down inside us, it's always been here.
   Keep lamps always trimmed and the flame burning bright,
   seize life in the daytime and walk to the light.

2. Consciousness slowly develops in us,
   we learn as we grow in both stillness and fuss.
   The oil we are burning brings light to this place,
   we grow self-aware more as we give Spirit space.

3. Let's not be foolish but belong to the wise,
   ensuring we always have all the supplies
   we need to grow wiser, and ever aware,
   so when we are called, we are ready and there.

4. Let us be present, alert every day,
   so we do not miss Life's lovely treasures this way.
   Let's pay full attention so consciousness grows,
   and spread the enchantment so ev'ryone knows.

Tune: Slane
(WOV 445)

O when I see the awesome world
A hymn of gratitude

1. O when I see the awesome world around me,
   and think of all the worlds which lie beyond;
   I see bright stars, I see the circling planets,
   auroras' shimmer, north and south's display.

   > *Then sings my soul, in gratitude and praise,*
   > *How great this world, the expanse of space.*
   > *Then sings my soul, in gratitude and praise,*
   > *How great this world, the expanse of space!*

2. When Matariki climbs above the skyline,
   shining its starlight o'er this lovely land.
   The old year done, a new year rises for us,
   remembering, rejoice on every hand.

   > *Then sings my soul, in gratitude and praise,*
   > *Bring the year in, let's start anew.*
   > *Then sings my soul, in gratitude and praise,*
   > *Bring the year in, let's start anew!*

3. And when I think, that deep inside the atom
   are bosons, quarks, invisible to me;
   My mind gropes for ability to grasp it,
   this nano-world, so packed with energy.

   > *Then sings my soul, in gratitude and praise,*
   > *Such precious life, such energy!*
   > *Then sings my soul, in gratitude and praise,*
   > *Such precious life, such energy!*

Tune: How Great Thou Art
(CH4 154, WOV 628)

Matariki is the Māori festival of the new year signalled by the reappearance of Matariki (the Pleiades) in the southern hemisphere. The first and third verses can also be sung at other times of the year.

On our life's journey

A hymn for all prodigals

1. On our life's journey we may take different ways;
   at one time content to stay home every day,
   at other moments a restlessness calls,
   we leave home and loved ones, hoping to 'have a ball'.

2. Life in the world is exciting and fun,
   we have new adventures, 'tick off' what we've done,
   we grow and develop, we learn more each day,
   but then, in an instant, find we're lost on the way.

3. Losing the signposts that show where to go
   causes our equilibrium to cease its flow;
   we lose all our bearings, start wondering why,
   and like many lost ones, feel we're in a pigsty.

4. Those desp'rate moments, deep in darkness profound,
   give quiet in which we can check, and re-sound
   the depths of the waters in which we could drown,
   and rescue ourselves, make it out to dry ground.

5. Even in pigsties we can find commonsense,
   and remember the Love which is given, not lent.
   We know there is welcome at home's open gate;
   we know we can go there, it is never too late.

Tune: Slane
(WOV 445)

Onward sacred pilgrims

A hymn about journeying together

1. Onward sacred pilgrims, seeking to engage
   with our mentor Jesus on his pilgrimage.
   He, the trusted leader, leads against the flow;
   forward to engagement, onward let us go.

   Onward sacred pilgrims!
   Seeking to engage,
   With our mentor, Jesus,
   Write a brand new page.

2. If we are authentic, darkness will retreat.
   Walk then, sacred pilgrims, walk with high intent.
   False foundations quiver at this sign of strength;
   Pilgrims, lift your voices, assent and dissent!

   Onward sacred pilgrims!
   Seeking to engage,
   With our mentor, Jesus,
   Write a brand new page.

3. Like a pilgrim people moves the church on earth;
   Pilgrims we are treading where the church made birth.
   We are not divided; all including, we;
   One in trust and one in love, one in diversity.

   Onward sacred pilgrims!
   Seeking to engage,
   With our mentor, Jesus,
   Write a brand new page.

4. Onward then all people, join our happy throng.
   Blend with ours your voices in reflective song.
   Celebration, love and peace for all humankind,
   and a great compassion, may all people find.

   Onward sacred pilgrims!
   Seeking to engage,
   With our mentor, Jesus,
   Write a brand new page.

Tune: St Gertrude
(BHB 520)

Our delight is in the broadness
A hymn of delight in the world

1. Our delight is in the broadness
   of the world dawn brings to sight;
   Harbour, beach and islands' structure,
   plain and hilltop, mountains' might;
   Thanks be giv'n for nature's beauty,
   celebrate each new day's light.

2. Our delight is in the living
   of each moment every day,
   working, playing, walking, sleeping,
   being family, straight, bi, gay;
   Grace be giv'n for every minute,
   wisdom for each interplay.

3. Our delight is in the springtime
   plants which decorate our view;
   Jonquils, blossom, tulips, crocus,
   gardens filled with colours new.
   Thanks to God for every petal,
   celebrate the God of hue.

4. Our delight is in the sharing
   with all creatures, this our place;
   moths and birds with stunning markings,
   dolphins moving with sweet grace;
   Thanks be giv'n for all creation,
   celebrate each life, each space.

5. Our delight is in the loving
   of each other, as we may;
   Searching, finding, liking, loving,
   talking, list'ning on the way;
   Thanks be giv'n for our affections,
   celebrate them night and day.

Tune: Praise, My Soul
(WOV 68)

Rainbow God

A hymn for the rainbow community

1. Rainbow God above us, arching down to us here
   where we live on the earth, this our home which is dear.
   Full beauty surrounds us, light shines bright and clear;
   Hail and glad hosanna, great and colourful God

2. Darkest, deep matter, holding life so serene,
   known only in action, but not fully seen.
   Our universe anchor holds fast all we've been;
   Hail and glad Hosanna, dark, mysterious God.

3. Bursting supernova, throwing stardust up high,
   shining brightly and lighting up all of the sky,
   illumining darkness, guide us as we sigh;
   Hail and glad hosanna, bright starburst, our God.

4. Red names our passion and orange is warm,
   bright yellow arrives with the hope of new dawn,
   green-blue shines our world, purple is royal-born;
   Hail and glad Hosanna, arching rainbow, our God.

Tune: Slane
(WOV 445)

So many times

A hymn expressing awe and wonder

1. So many times, I gaze in awe and wonder,
   as our blue earth hangs silently in space.
   I see the stars, their ancient light, still moving
   t'wards me now, truth I almost can't face.

   > O mighty world, my heart cries loud and free,
   > How great this is, this universe!
   > Let my praise sound for you both loud and free,
   > How great this world, for all, and me!

2. Great solar power beams forth upon our planet,
   Maintaining life, an energetic base.
   The planets orbit on their different axes,
   and stars adorn the inky black of space

   > O mighty world, my heart cries loud and free,
   > How great this is, this universe!
   > Let my praise sound for you both loud and free,
   > How great this world, for all, and me!

3. And deep inside, where human eye can't follow
   are gluons, quarks, so small we can't see.
   Black holes create mysterious deep dark hollows,
   dark matter holds us all invisibly.

   > O mighty world, my heart cries loud and free,
   > How great this is, this universe!
   > Let my praise sound for you both loud and free,
   > How great this world, for all, and me!

4. So each is valued, big and microscopic,
   all play a part in one dramatic act.
   So each of us, unknown or mildly famous,
   Are welcome, each of universe a part.

   > O mighty world, my heart cries loud and free,
   > How great this is, this universe!
   > Let my praise sound for you both loud and free,
   > How great this world, for all, and me!

Tune: How Great Thou Art
(CH4 154, WOV 628)

The church needs a foundation
A hymn for the postmodern church

1. The church needs a foundation,
   Though not of brick or stone
   For buildings are but shelter,
   From rain or hailstorm.
   They symbolise commitment,
   They resonate with praise,
   But humans form the true church
   In these postmodern days.

2. Through Christendom's great worship
   The rafters have been wrung,
   We've gazed at stained glass windows,
   Made sure the brass has shone.
   We've consecrated, maintained,
   We've renovated, but
   Religion's modern rituals,
   Are those postmoderns cut.

3. The commonwealth of spirit
   Is not built out of wood.
   But by our follow'ng Jesus
   with praxis that is good.
   Postmodern 'church' emerges
   In fresh expressions, new,
   With talk and acts of justice,
   Compassion, which is true.

4. In our time now, we follow
   Jesus upon the Way,
   On terms for us authentic,
   And honest for this day.
   We see our 'church' re-forming,
   the Spirit helps it grow;
   We see again, a future
   Where faith will always flow.

Tune: Aurelia
(WOV 385)

The Treaty came here for the signing

A hymn for the anniversary of the Wellington signing of the Treaty of Waitangi on 29 April 1840.

1. The Treaty came here for the signing,
   From Waitangi to the Cook Strait,
   And Williams called for Rangatira,[2]
   To make their mark in their place.
   How do we live as two peoples?
   Sharing the land and the sea?
   How do we honour the Treaty,
   And legislate for sovereignty?

2. The twenty-ninth day of that April,
   The year eighteen forty, they signed.
   The thirty-two-strong Rangatira,
   With multiple questions in mind:
   How do we live as two peoples?
   Sharing the land and the sea?
   Will these men honour the Treaty,
   And maintain our sovereignty?

3. The harbour surrounded the party,
   Its hills as yet unmarked with homes.
   The chorus of birds loud and lovely,
   Trees standing, green, living poems.
   How do we live as two peoples?
   Sharing the land and the sea?
   How can we honour the Treaty,
   And care for this land and this sea?

4. Today others too now have joined us,
   Skin colour is of every hue,
   This land and this sea must support us,
   How can we care for them too?
   Our history's not one that we're proud of,
   The Treaty's been a battleground,
   Ignored, forgotten, dishonoured,
   But now let us turn that around.

---

2   *Rangatira* is a Māori word meaning chief

Let's all treat each other with justice,
and care for this land and this sea.
Let all of us honour the Treaty,
so all can be equal and free.

Tune: Let justice roll down (Waitaki)
(AA 85)

The woman came

A hymn about encounter

1. The woman came along that day
   for water from the well.
   The other women had gone home,
   they didn't want to know her well,
   she was left out, all alone,
   she was left out, alone.

2. She found a stranger sitting there,
   on her well's stony rim.
   He was a man, and she was not,
   she didn't think she'd talk to him,
   he and her sort didn't talk,
   he and her sort don't talk.

3. But they discussed, and argued long
   on water, life, and prayer.
   He challenged her, she challenged him,
   they met, connected then right there;
   Things would never be the same,
   they'd never be the same.

4. We do not know what encounters wait
   to meet us on our way.
   How strangers can reset our lives,
   how we can learn anew each day
   that the Spirit is within,
   the Spirit is within.

Tune: Repton
(WOV 519 (ii))

The year is ever turning

A hymn of the year and the journey

1. The year is ever turning, Spring welcomes back the light.
   The heat of summer fades, then in autumn birds take flight.
   In winter, darkness closes and temp'ratures grow chill,
   Yet warmth will always be ours, for love is primary still.

2. Among New Zealand's foothills our hearts are overcome,
   The stars and planets tell us creating's never done;
   Aurora (the australis) streaks through the evening sky;
   At this, like Spirit's myst'ry, we question "How?" and "Why?"

3. In bright sunlight we wander on hill and track and road;
   Walking with one another we carry each one's load;
   Tall tussocks brush our ankles, steep gradients test our heart,
   The journey takes us onward; of cosmos, we are part.

4. These days, we now can gather in café, candled halls,
   Churches not yet familiar or where we first were called;
   Together now, we stumble t'wards love below, above,
   Beside us and behind us, surrounding, all is Love.

Tune: Ewing
(WOV 346)

Note: While this is a specifically New Zealand hymn, you might be able to replace the word New Zealand with something appropriate and in the northern hemisphere replace 'the australis' with 'borealis'. The word 'Tussocks' can be replaced with 'grasses.'

Through the crowds

A Hymn for Palm Sunday

1. Through the crowds a donkey passes,
   Grey and humble, young and small.
   Makes its way among the masses
   Carrying Jesus through it all;
   Quietly, gently, rides the stranger,
   Loud and boisterous is the crowd,
   Calm and centred, into danger,
   Sure his pathway to his shroud.

2. Symbols seen at every corner,
   Coats and donkeys, stones and palms.
   Raucous joy, no sadness or mourners,
   Spirits high, with ringing psalms;
   Simple triumph is all their agenda,
   Welcoming a King above kings.
   Not a thought of evil offender,
   Streets with glad hosannas ring.

3. In our lives we face such choices,
   Which the leader we will choose?
   Here one whom the crowd rejoices,
   Over there, one bound to lose;
   One has riches and prestige and power,
   One has only love to expend;
   Every day and even each hour,
   We decide which we'll befriend.

4. May we find the courage to ponder
   Not the easy, but the best;
   In our hearts, make room for wonder,
   Find, through myst'ry, the truest quest
   Which demands the fullest commitment,
   Life and love, possessions too,
   Heart and mind both fully recruited,
   All now making a journey true.

Tune: Blaenwern
(WOV 165 (ii))

Susan Jones

To the wilderness so hostile

1. To the wilderness so hostile,
   Hagar went with Abram's son.
   Sent in shame, her mistress cursing,
   suffered they under hot sun.
   She seemed destined for oblivion,
   but she wasn't there alone,
   but she wasn't there alone.

2. For a long time Israel wandered,
   through the Sinai's desert paths.
   Egypt's bonds were looking better,
   every aching step they passed.
   But they made their destination,
   living, loving there anew,
   living, loving there anew.

3. To the desert, hot and thirsty,
   Jesus was compelled to go.
   Still warmed by the water's blessing,
   there he found he faced a foe.
   He rejected fame and glory,
   for his goal was only truth,
   for his goal was only truth.

4. Solo mother, ancient people,
   novice teacher, looked for help.
   Spirit of the wilderness and desert,
   help us find our inner Self.
   In the dust and thirst and hunger,
   may we hear that inner voice,
   may we hear that inner voice.

Tune: Cwm Rhondda
(WOV 478)

We bring thankful hearts
A hymn of thanksgiving

1. We bring thankful hearts for energy, for youthfulness and age,
   For friends and home and family, for innocent and sage,
   For sporting life and too for stillness, for silence and for sound,
   For drama and reflection and singers of renown,
   For all the world's enrichment, its culture, spirit true,
   For being alive in all of it, being on the Way with you.

2. We are those who have experienced the loss and pain of fear,
   When world and home and families by trauma have been seared.
   We are thankful now for comfort, giv'n then by friendship true,
   When days were dark and dreary, so we still made it through,
   And we're glad that Jesus knows well how life us all can sway,
   Sharing with us every dark time, stay'ng with us on the Way.

3. And now we face the future, where meaning may be found.
   Seeking lives that work on justice, that stand on solid ground.
   We all want to make a difference, so this world will still survive
   And be a place where peace is, where children stay alive.
   As we all walk on together, may Love be here each day,
   And may our lives be worthwhile, as people of the Way.

Tune: Thaxted
(BHB 642)

We give praise for the river's flow

1. We give praise for the river's flow,
   And all the waters here below,
   Praise the creative voice, once heard,
   When waters' chaos were disturbed.

2. Long rivers flowing o'er the plains,
   Provide our lifeblood, bring us gain.
   May all the waters on the earth,
   Be giv'n by humans their true worth.

3. The flow of fluid waters may
   Throw all our plans, to disarray,
   For pow'rful waters flood us too
   Disturbing, changing, settled views.

4. Thirst quenching streams speak of great Love:
   Their length, the distance Love will move
   To reach our hearts, and save our soul,
   To feed us richly, make us whole.

5. White waters tumble with great joy,
   May our praise be no flippant ploy
   To glibly please; instead, let's vow
   To raft with Love, embarking now.

Tune: Gonfalon Royal
(WOV 318)

We thank the men and women

A hymn for all brave people

1. We thank the men and women,
   who bring the Christ to birth,
   both hidden and identified,
   in past and present earth;
   Who feed and clothe, and water
   all children of the womb,
   and strive to make a home for them,
   from dawn, through night and noon.

2. Bathsheba was disrupted,
   from marriage to the throne;
   And Tamar found, when widowed,
   she suddenly was alone;
   Rahab was brave, when Joshua
   put Jericho under threat;
   Ruth changed her country, followed love,
   gleaned well, so safety met.

3. We all face times of turmoil too,
   and questions that are hard;
   Complex decisions try our hearts,
   allegiances are marred;
   Whatever gender, we decide
   whom we call friend, or foe;
   Let's call on Love to reconcile,
   to Fear, let us say "No!"

Tune: Ellacombe
(WOV 277)

What does it mean?
A hymn for gender equality

1. What does it mean to be a woman?
   Are they meant to be 'sugar and spice'?
   When a female is in charge,
   Do we think that's not quite nice?
   If a girl becomes the leader,
   or a woman takes public role,
   what do we think of how she should do that?
   What expectations do we hold?

2. How should a man be truly masc'line?
   What are attributes he should show?
   When a man is called to be gentle,
   Do we think that's not the right flow?
   If a man likes only to follow,
   or prefers a nurturing role,
   what do we think of how he should do that?
   What expectations do we hold?

3. Deb'rah was a prophet in Israel,
   So were Samuel, Elijah and John;
   Jael killed in definite fashion,
   So did Joshua, David, and Saul.
   David took in Jonathan's son,
   Jesus called little children to come;
   Is it our gender which should define us?
   Or the right actions we each have done?

4. Let us cease dividing and conq'ring.
   Let us help every person, to choose
   the whole range of human reactions,
   skills, accomplishments; nothing to lose.
   Women, men, those fluid of gender,
   each one choosing anew each day.
   Let all respond, with ready obedience,
   to Life's true call and to Life's true Way.

Tune: Abbot's Leigh
(WOV 93)

When I walk through bush so green
A hymn of gratitude for creation

1. When I walk through bush so green, so luscious,
   Ferns layered under tall tree canopies;
   And see the birds, each in its niche for living,
   And hear the sounds of birdsongs, rustling leaves.

   Then sings my soul, in gratitude and praise,
   How great this world, this green life here.
   Then sings my soul, in gratitude and praise,
   How great this world, this green life here!

2. O when I see the awesome world around me,
   and think of all the worlds which lie beyond;
   I see bright stars, I see the circling planets,
   auroras' shimmer, north and south's display.

   Then sings my soul, in gratitude and praise,
   How great this world, the expanse of space.
   Then sings my soul, in gratitude and praise,
   How great this world, the expanse of space!

3. This precious earth, our nest in which we flourish,
   Is crucial to our happiness and health;
   Can we co-operate with one another,
   To make it truly all our common wealth?

   So sings my soul, let's act now on our praise,
   How great this world, let's save it now,
   Then sings my soul, our energy to raise,
   How great this world, let's save it now!

   Tune: How Great Thou Art
   (CH4 154, WOV 628)

When we were young our God was huge
A hymn of faith stages

1. When we were young our God was huge,
   grey bearded, distant, tall;
   He ruled the earth and knew each move,
   judged all, both great and small.

2. We learned of Love shown by the man,
   who walked here long ago,
   but others blotted out, with guilt,
   the peace we longed to know.

3. Then as we grew we changed our view,
   we questioned, thought and prayed;
   Our God became less gruff and cold,
   her colours more displayed.

4. So we have learned, that God is like
   a rainbow in the sky,
   embracing many different hues,
   straight, trans and gay and bi.

5. A rainbow God is colourful,
   accepting, bright and gay;
   Like joy which shines right through the rain,
   Joy which won't go away.

Tune: Amazing Grace
(WOV 56)

When life is filled with logic

A hymn about Transfiguration

1. When life is filled with logic, reason fair,
   scripture confronts us with a scene bizarre;
   Can we believe this moment is for real?
   Can we believe, and preach with ready zeal?

2. Then we remember moments just like this;
   when, too, we tapped a vein into the depths,
   arrested then by glory breaking fair,
   our hearts burst open with a 'knowing' clear.

3. Everyday things, transfigured by great love,
   bathed in the sunshine which seemed from above,
   causing that love to dance within all things,
   and joy inspired our rational minds to sing.

4. May we be helped to trust and to be wise,
   to see right through the mundane, with new eyes,
   even here now, in our postmodern times,
   may we allow light in us to arise.

Tune: Woodlands
(WOV 109)

Susan Jones

Where can we learn greater loving?

A wedding hymn for Henry and Keith

1. Where can we learn greater loving,
   than our tiny selves can show?
   Who displays the faithful living,
   which we long, each day, to know?

2. Look at Jesus, grace-filled, living
   out on earth, the love we need;
   Look at all creation's beauty,
   shaped by loving Creativity.

3. See the Spirit holds together,
   Creator and earth-bound Son,
   mystic union binds each other
   to the next, here's how love is done.

4. This our guide then, this our model,
   Loves creates, guides, and empowers.
   In our human lives we're helped, to
   nurture love each day and every hour

5. God-infused, Love lasts forever,
   Jesus shows how that can be,
   Spirit energises, maintains
   in us, fragrant love eternally.

6. May your love glint bright like stardust,
   may your days be Spirit-fired,
   Love each other, gently, firmly,
   Let Christ all your ways inspire.

Tune: The Servant Song
(CH4 694, TIS 650)

Work for the night is here
A hymn for the endangered species in Aotearoa New Zealand

1. Work for the night is here, extinction hovers close,
   in Aotearoa's sphere birds are at risk. The most:
   Our rivers' Small Black Stilt, and Kakapo's bright green,
   The Taiko, Heron, (white), and Fairy Tern are little seen.

2. Work for the shades close in on species large and small.
   Some hide, or swim seas out and in, some elegant, some tall:
   The Greater Short Tailed bat, our Sea Lions are quite few,
   The South'rn Elephant Seal and Maui's dolphin, Bryde's whale, too.

3. Life is a precious thing, let's treat all with great care.
   The creatures of this world depend on us to keep life fair.
   The mandate has been giv'n; to care, to till, to mend;
   As stewards of this lovely place, all creatures we befriend.

4. Some species are at risk, and more need safety too,
   from predator's greed and human need;
   what is the best to do?
   We co-create this world by how we treat all life,
   the web of our relationships deserves we care and strive.

5. Delicate, fragile, frayed, the web of life shows wear.
   Some links still hold, be not afraid, instead, become aware;
   There is no magic wand, which waved, can make all right,
   unless we humans, you and I, turn species' night to light.

Tune: Diademata
(WOV 163)

While this hymn is specific to Aotearoa New Zealand, the last 3 verses could be sung on their own in other countries.

Hymn Indexes

Topics and Themes

Bible
- Ancient words ring through the aeons 16
- From ancient times the stories flowed 26
- Guide me now to climb the mountain 28
- Letters written to the churches 38
- On our life's journey 42

Children
- A wise poet wrote one day 14

Church
- I sing a song of the saints of God 29
- The church needs a foundation 47

Communion
- As we meet 18
- Each Lent we journey with a much-loved friend 22

Gender Equality
- We thank the men and women 56
- What does it mean? 57

Inner Journey
- And did those feet in former times 17
- A wise poet wrote one day 14
- It takes us effort 37
- Let us reach down deep inside us 39
- Now comes the bridegroom 40
- On our life's journey 42
- Onward sacred pilgrims 43
- The woman came 50
- Through the crowds 52
- To the wilderness so hostile 53
- We bring thankful hearts 54
- We thank the men and women 56
- When life is filled with logic 60
- When we were young our God was huge 59

Marriage
- Where can we learn greater loving? 61

Matariki
- O when I see the awesome world 41

Offering
- It takes us effort 37

Questioning/Growing in Faith
    A wise poet wrote one day 14
    For all the saints (2) 24

Tragedy
    Celebrate the life we're given (3) 21

Treaty of Waitangi
    The Treaty came here for the signing 48

Bible References

John 4: The woman came 50
Luke 15: On our life's journey 42
Matthew 17: When life is filled with logic 60
Matthew 25: Now comes the bridegroom 40
Psalm 8: O when I see the awesome world 41

The Church Year

Advent
    A donkey walks his burden 12
    Ancient words ring through the aeons 16
    It takes us effort 37
    We thank the men and women 56

Creation
    In our world we find delight 31, 34
    Our delight is in the broadness 44
    O when I see the awesome world 41
    So many times 46
    The year is ever turning 51
    We give praise for the river's flow 55
    When I walk through bush so green 58
    Work for the night is here 62

Easter
    Great is the glory of this newborn day 27

Lent
    And did those feet in former times 17
    Each Lent we journey with a much-loved friend 22

Palm Sunday
    Through the crowds 52

Pentecost
    Now comes the bridegroom 40
    The woman came 50

Special Sundays
Baptism
  Celebrate the Life we're given (1) 19
Church Anniversary
  All people that on earth do hear 15
Gender Identity/Roles
  We thank the men and women 56
  What does it mean? 57
Mothers' Day
  For all the saints (3) 25
Rainbow/Pride Festivals
  Celebrate the Life we're given (2) 20
  Rainbow God 45
Reformers' Sunday
  A safe stronghold we may seek still 13
  The church needs a foundation 47
Transgender Day of Remembrance
  For all the saints (1) 23

Tunes

Abbot's Leigh	(WOV 93)	57
Amazing Grace	(WOV 56)	59
Aurelia	(WOV 385)	47
Austria	(WOV 577)	19, 20, 21
Blaenwern	(WOV 165 (ii))	38, 52
Cwm Rhondda	(WOV 478)	28, 53
Diademata	(WOV 163)	62
Ein Feste Burg	(WOV 8)	13
Ellacombe	(WOV 277)	56
Ewing	(WOV 346)	51
Finlandia	(WOV 48)	22
Gaelic Traditional Melody	(FFS 10 (i))	39
Gentle Jesus	(WOV 545)	14
Gonfalon Royal	(WOV 318)	55
Grand Isle	(BHB 259, WOV 551)	30
How Great Thou Art	(CH4 154, WOV 628)	41, 46, 58
Hyfrydol	(WOV 173)	16
In our world we find delight		34
Jerusalem	(CH4 106)	17
Langran	(CH4 664 (a), HTC 406)	18
Let justice roll down (Waitaki)	(AA 85)	49
Lucerna Laudoniae	(WOV 77)	26
Maccabaeus	(WOV 303)	27
Nos Galan (Deck the Halls with Boughs of Holly)		12
Old 100th	(WOV 10)	15

Praise, My Soul	(WOV 68)	44
Repton	(WOV 519 (ii))	50
Sine Nomine	(WOV 384)	23, 24, 25
Slane	(WOV 445)	37, 40, 42, 45
St Gertrude	(BHB 520)	43
Thaxted	(BHB 642)	54
The Servant Song	(CH4 694, TIS 650)	61
Woodlands	(WOV 109)	60

Wording our Worship — New words for new ideas

1 — Responsive Gatherings

Gathering for the First Sunday in Advent
Advent 1 Year C

Today we begin the advent journey to Bethlehem
We find travelling with us,
parents-to-be, shepherds and wise ones.

Energised by Hope, we know something momentous is happening
Let hearts be open and minds alert, ears listening
Let Hope have its advent into the world
again and again and again.

Gathering for the Second Sunday in Advent
Advent 2 Year B

We gather to continue our Advent journey.
Facing challenges old and new
We follow a pathway through darkness to light.
Let us travel this pathway together.

Springtime blossom transforms into new leaves and fruit
and crimson sprinkles of pohutukawa emerge from tiny buds.
We watch as the Advent candle of Hope shines brightly
within the wreath.
Let us watch and wait together.
Let us watch and wait with hope.

As we continue our journey to Bethlehem
gale force winds are calmed into gentle zephyr breezes.
White capped waves settle into sparkling ripples on our harbour
We watch as the Advent candle of Peace gleams
within the wreath.
Let us watch and wait together.
Let us watch and wait for peace.

Gathering for the Fourth Sunday in Advent
Advent 4 Year C

The mystery draws nearer to our heart's core
The timeless cycle of birth beginning a new era.

The timeless image of love born in lowly origins
The timeless images of love curling trusting fingers around ours.

Who knows when and how this first happened?
We only know it is happening now. Deck the halls!

Gathering for Christmas Eve
Christmas Eve Year C

On such a night as this the mystery of birth happened
This time, we are told, among animals of the earth.

Sometimes, children are born more comfortably, often less so
Mother and child form a new bond, families grow.

Fathers rejoice and worry about the future
All the drama of life is here, on such a night as this.

Gathering for the Third Sunday in Lent
Lent 3 Year A

The Lenten journey continues
We walk with Jesus this path of danger and risk.

Along the way we are meeting with others
Those who walked the path with him as we do now.

Jesus himself in desert conditions, dazzled disciples,
an estranged Samaritan, a man born blind and his family,
and two grieving sisters,
And then the usual Holy Week crowd,
A motley company of people much like us.

Different time and place, but our common humanity the same.
We all are welcome as we walk this Lenten path together.

Gathering for the Fourth Sunday in Lent
Lent 4 Year C

Finding your way is a tricky task
Sometimes we lose our direction.

Markers don't have the same meaning or have disappeared
Is being lost a sin or simply part of our human journey?

Gathering for the Fifth Sunday in Lent
Lent 5 Year C

We continue our journey of life and growth
Pondering what we need to die to
in order to live for something else.

What does it mean to fall into the ground?
What does it mean to let go?
What would new growth mean on this journey of life?

Gathering for Palm Sunday
Palm Sunday Year B

The journey to Jerusalem has been accomplished
Jesus arrives in a space of quiet within a cacophony of sound.

Our journey is ongoing
Where is the space of quiet in us among the noise of life?

Gathering for After Easter Day
After Easter Year C

What do you do after the world has ended?
How do you carry on?

What do we do now our world has changed?
Do we carry on?

What and who is calling us into the future?
Do we follow the call?

How will the church emerge from this transition?
We are the ones who will decide.

Gathering for Pentecost

Pentecost Year A

The Spirit is abroad, about in our world!
Dazzling with fire, breathing new life into old ways;

Never something we can fully explain
But always bringing Life and Creativity.

We celebrate this day we have named the birthday of the Church
When new life and energy were birthed among us.

New life and energy are still needed now and here.
May we have courage in the face of such disruptive Love.

Gathering to Consider Grace

Ordinary Time Year C

We gather to ascribe worth
to all that is of ultimate concern to us;
Love and Shalom,
community and grace,
the sacred and secular.

We gather so this space, prayed in for so many years,
is graced again and again with divine intention
and human attention to what is significant,
graced by creativity,
paired with wisdom,
breathed into by Spirit.

We set aside this special time,
in this holy place made for now and always.
In this familiar place,
we see the beauty of grace,
we feel the shalom of love.

Gathering to Consider Action
Ordinary Time Year C

We can talk up a storm about what we think
We can think a lot in our heads about how we see the world.

We can write statements of aspiration and intention
None of this matters very much if we do nothing
If good people just sit on their hands, evil will flourish.

We may delight in being orthodox progressives
We need to also exercise orthopraxy
So what we believe is reflected in what we do
This is the Way Jesus took.
This is the Way in which we walk.

Gathering to Consider Spirituality
Ordinary Time Year C

Spirituality sometimes cannot be expressed in words,
but can be danced through our world,
painted in shapes and swirls and squares.

The Spirit may be found in dramatic moments;
Through music it whispers its way to our heart.

Walking in the creative steps of The Creator,
we become co-creators of beauty and form,
of colour and movement;
through all forms of the arts, thus we find our spirits nourished.

Thanks be given for this sweet and challenging beauty.
Thanks be given for creativity.

Gathering to Consider Faith
Ordinary Time Year C

Faith seeks understanding so our minds are brought into play
Do our experiences need words to be passed on as wisdom?

How do we understand what is happening around us
By experience, then thought, then action, then reflection;

Body mind and spirit all play their part
Entwining together to help us to be whole, complete, human beings.

Gathering to Consider the Inner Journey
Ordinary Time Year B
We have a journey to make
An inner journey circling deep within in labyrinthine style.
We do not need external armour
But internal preparation which protects and guides
as we step further on the journey the ancients followed,
continuing it in our time.

Gathering to Consider Life's Rhythm
After Easter Year C

What is the rhythm of our lives?
Is there presence and balance?

Accountability as well as creativity?
Acceptance and hospitality?

Are our lives marked by a rhythm of prayer
Or by panicky heartbeats?

What rhythm do we choose?
What is the background beat to the music of our lives?

Gathering for Creation Month
Creation Year C

We enter the month of Creation Sundays
celebrating oceans and storms, cosmos and creatures;

We ponder in awe the complexity of this planet
and wonder with grief at the destruction being wrought upon it.

May we not stop at simple admiration
but act to reverse damage already done.

May we not stop at our use of the earth's resources
but act to ensure no more wounding of this living planet.

May this bright blue teardrop, hanging in vast heavens
always pulse freely with life and love.

Gathering for Cosmos Sunday
Creation 4 Year C

The cosmos can be very, very large
and can be very, very small.

From supernovae and giant nebula in the universe's skies
To quarks and gluons at the atomic level
Its realities baffle and defeat scientific minds
Its beauty defies the skill of artists and poets
Its scale amazes the human mind.

Who are we that any divinity in the world
might be mindful of us or visit us?

Yet we are loved, welcomed and accepted into this world
This world which stretches from visible stars and planets,
to invisible particles and electrons. Amen.

Gathering for Reformers' Sunday
Ordinary Time Year C

Over half a millennium ago, reformers spoke up
and both church and world changed.

Now in our time, we face a point of discernment.
We are the actors now; will we be reformers or resisters?

As for them, now for us, how do we discern the way forward?
We are the ones called to decide
when to be literal and when to embrace the mythical,
when to be logical and when to embrace the mystical.

This is the time of the Great Emergence,
may we act so that in this time, great things will emerge.

Gathering in an Inclusive Church
Ordinary Time Year C

All are welcome here
Easily said, but taking more effort in practice.

All are welcome here
**Not just the fashionable in group which needs support
but also the regular, the ordinary, the sometimes irritating ones.**

All are welcome here
**Even those who do not fall into any listed category
All are welcome here.**

Gathering for Transgender Sunday
Ordinary Time Year C

All human beings are valuable
simply because they are human.

All human beings are worth loving
simply because they are human.

Whether we understand another or not,
whether they are different or not,
they are due respect and the expectation of life.

All human beings are due unconditional love.
**All humankind, all orientations, all genders, all people,
are welcome here.**

So may it always be
Amen.

Gathering for Transgender Day of Remembrance
Ordinary Time Year C

Whatever the language, Love is the word which binds us to each other
Whatever language we know, Love is the context in which we gather.

However we name it, Love is what holds us together
However we may seek to hide, Love searches until we are found.

Love conquers all
And the truth will set us free.

So may it be
Amen.

Gathering of a Welcoming Church
Ordinary Time Year B

In this place all are welcome
The tall, the thin, the shy and the 'out there.'

In this place all are accepted
Cis and trans, gay, lesbian, straight and bisexual.

In this place all are loved
Simply because we are all human beings.

In this place all are honoured
For the struggle between commemoration and celebration goes on for all of us all the time.

Gathering of an Inclusive Church
Ordinary Time Year B

Everyone on this earth is covered by the sky
All humankind lives their life covered by the same canopy.

The rain falls on just and unjust
The sun shines on all colours and shades of people.

We are sisters and brothers and kin living together
on this sky-surrounded home
We are family, we are one.

Gathering for Pride Sunday
Lent Year C

All colours of the earth enrich our life
exciting red, fresh orange and bright yellow
new green, calm blue and regal violet
All unite in a rainbow of promise and hope
So we can become one together, with the rainbow God.

Gathering for an Inclusive Service
After Easter Year B

How can I be honest to now?
How can I be honest to both divinity and humanity?

How can I become honest?
How can I become honest to both divinity and humanity?

How are people included in ways they appreciate?
How do I like to be included? Are others the same?

Including, becoming, is a hard road
And the journey on which everyone is invited.

Gathering for Pride Week
Lent Year C

We celebrate our many identities,
all human beings, colouring the planet;
Multicoloured, multi-orientated, multi-generational.
We seek the truth for today
so we can be one company of pilgrims together
in love and trust and solidarity of faith.

Gathering on Communion Sunday
Ordinary Time Year C

Today we reflect on the act of Communion
Communion over a meal;

Communion in prayer
Communing when in silence and
Communion conveyed by words.

Let us reach deep within
and learn more about ourselves.

Gathering on Communion Sunday
Ordinary Time Year C

We gather around the table
Seeking a community based on love.

We welcome whanau to this place
They seek a community based on love.

We will leave today and go out of these doors
Seeking to create and recreate communities of love.

Gathering for Refugee Sunday
Ordinary Time Year C

This day we remember refugees,
those displaced and homeless, as Jesus' story tells us he was.

A refugee baby, he fled with his parents to Egypt,
long-time refuge for Jews in trouble.

We think of families
displaced by war and famine and oppression of different kinds,
going where people do not want them,

living in exile where they do not want to be,
longing to return home.

May we learn this day what that is like
so we have empathy for those who are displaced.

Gathering During Bible Month
Ordinary Time Year C

You never know who you might meet at the water cooler
When you are in the middle of your daily routine.

Let us dip down deep into the heart of ourselves
**And find what was always there,
waiting for us to re-discover it.**

So may it be
Amen.

Gathering During Bible Month
Ordinary Time Year C

We gather for community and for the grace of sacred presence.
We sit and work, we pray and prepare.

We can get very busy even on this sacred day.
We can miss the quiet moment when all comes together.

Let us, this day, pay attention to what is important.
Everything is important, in its own moment.

2 — Pairs of Responsive Gatherings and Affirmations

Gathering After a General Election
In light of these political times, an elected office just inaugurated,
we consider how ethical and spiritually mature leadership
can be found in our world, here and abroad.
Alternative visions or 'alternative facts'?
Beatitudes, manifestos, policies, personalities…

How can everything be brought together,
So all can live in a commonwealth of justice and peace?

Affirmation for a New Era

We affirm this world is made for all people,
that the pursuit of health and happiness
is both the right of all and the responsibility of all.

We recall Jesus always looked for the best in those he met
urging people to go a second mile
and for honesty in our dealings with each other.

We recall he saw beyond wealth and privilege
to what would satisfy the soul.
We recall he lived out Micah's call to seek justice,
love mercy, and walk humbly on the earth.

We believe we are called to emulate his actions and attitude,
to be people of integrity,
working for the long term good of our community and nation
and the lasting good of this planet.

We affirm, as vital tools to those ends,
the importance of hope and of faith and of love
for all people, in each country on this earth.

Gathering for a Questioning People
Epiphany Year C

As we struggle to know what to believe
We question what it is to walk the path of life.

As we struggle to know who and what to trust
We question what it is to follow the spiritual journey.

As we struggle to know in who or what to have faith
We question where we will take the next footstep.

Affirmation of Faith
(Please join in with as much of the affirmation as you can.)

We trust in Life which never ends.
A flowing, underground aquifer of life,
refreshing and nourishing
all those who root themselves in its cool clear water.

**We yearn for greening
to spring forth from this Source of Life,
new growth unfolding in human hearts,
despite the drought-stricken deserts which lie around them
and the heart-stopping, bitter cold of evil greed.**

We trust that deep down inside us
the aquifer of life flows unendingly,
unpolluted and magnificent,
delicately whispering its loving way
when our wounds need the salve of fresh hope.

**We seek the grace to plant ourselves beside
and in this sacred stream of living water
so we too may bear fruit in the season to come.**

Gathering During Pride Month
Lent Year C

We join in familiarity and community
We welcome visitors and new associations.

Today we begin the month which celebrates 'Pride' and 'Festival'
We join this celebration of being human and being free.

May this freedom be available for all orientations, races and people
**May our goal be friendship amongst those who are different,
in the same way Jesus befriended all.**

Affirmation for an Inclusive Church

The doors of this church are open to all,
just as Jesus welcomed all kinds and types of people
we seek to keep doors and arms open wide.

**We believe that the love of God,
as expressed in the life of Jesus,
now is available to all through the Spirit.**

We celebrate the red of passion,
warm orange of sunrise, bright yellow of hope,
we yearn for the greenness of new life
the clear blue of overarching love
and share the royal, purple status of being children of God together.

**We give thanks that this is possible
through sacred human promise and everlasting divine love.**

Gathering for Palm Sunday

Palm Sunday Year C

Today we celebrate Jesus' pilgrimage to Jerusalem
Pilgrimages have changed over the millennia.

Transport has changed over the centuries
Warrior kings used horses, but Jesus used a donkey.

Privileged people use cars and buses and trains
Would Jesus arrive on a scooter if he were a pilgrim today?

Affirmation of Faith for Palm Sunday

(You are invited to join in with as much of this as you honestly can)

With stark symbolism we celebrate this journey:
Waving palms suggest popularity and endorsement
but for Jesus these will fade as the week draws on.
He walks on however, does not cut and run.

Without such stark symbolism
We face our many journeys within life.
We may seek popularity and endorsement.
They do not always come
or they fade as for Jesus that eventful week.

In this moment of truth,
we affirm our intention to always journey on
as far as we are humanly able.

In this moment of truth,
we affirm our intention not to cut and run
as far as we are humanly able.

In this moment of truth,
we face our own fallibility and express our desire
for the Spirit's strength, support, and courage
to bolster our human spirit so we can stay the distance.

Gathering for Pentecost

Pentecost Year B

As autumn flames into life
We celebrate the Spirit's fire.

Falling on the earth, leaves carpet the ground
Falling on the church, the Spirit warms each heart.

Spirit of truth and power
Spirit of light and love.

Come, Spirit, Come
The Spirit Has Come!

Now again in your different languages
The Spirit Has Come!

Affirmation at Pentecost

We believe Spirit-power colours our lives with light;

**We celebrate the crimson red of fire,
energy captured in bright yellows, warmth and brilliance in orange;**

We celebrate the boldness of blue
the significance of purple;

**We believe all fire's colours are present in our lives;
Lighting up corners, warming cold places;**

We rejoice that Spirit is with us this day;

**Thanks be given for
fire in our belly,
energy in our hearts,
vitality brought to our soul.**

So may it be.
Amen.

Gathering on Disability Sunday
Disability Sunday Year A

All are welcome here
Whatever their degree of ability or disability.

All are welcome here
whether exiled from home or on their own ground.

All are welcome here,
you are not alone.

Affirmation for Disability Sunday

All people are equal
Whatever challenges they face.

Some face the challenge of disability
their personhood can become fragile.

Some face the challenge of ability
and high expectations for achievement and success.

Some face the challenge
of assisting others to reach their full potential.

Some face the challenge of dislocation
and the need to adapt to new circumstance.

Some face the challenge of always having been at home
where they must work to keep themselves growing and refreshed.

Some face the challenge of coming and going
risking losing themselves.

We are all challenged, sometimes comfortably, sometimes not.
We equally share the goal of striving to be complete human beings, every day we can.

Gathering for a Series on Compassion[3]
Ordinary Time Year B

True compassion rises from our very depths
It is in the wrenching of the guts.

It springs from the labouring womb
It is born of internal struggle
In which true compassion births mercy.

As Jesus did, may we too be moved in our inner selves
And show divine compassion.

Affirmation for 1st Sunday in Series of Four on Compassion

We believe Compassion is the essence of what we call God,
the deep internal urge to care for all
to show mercy to those who need it
to show love whether the recipient deserves it or not,

that deep internal force which brings forth
new relationship
new covenants of truth and justice
new life in all its forms.

We believe that as God acts so should we,
showing compassion even
to those we do not like
to those whom we may fear
and those who may hate and revile us.

We believe Compassion is needed for a world which is just and true,
a deeply held feeling shown in acts of mercy and kindness.

---

[3] The affirmations created for this series of 4 services centring on Compassion have been drawn from the Charter for Compassion begun and promoted by Karen Armstrong.
The full Charter can be found at https://charterforcompassion.org/

Gathering for the Second Compassion Sunday
Ordinary Time Year B

Compassion springs from the Womb of Life in each of us
True compassion is passionate and emotional.

Today let us see what happens to others when compassion is missing
How we might act or speak without compassion.

True compassion acknowledges another's worth
**May we all embrace our common humanity
by showing divine compassion.**

Affirmation of Faith said as an Offering Prayer
We are called, all of us
**to restore compassion to the centre of morality and religion,
that compassion might be our goal.**

We are called, all of us
**to return to the ancient principle that
interpreting scripture in ways which breed violence,
hatred, or disdain
is illegitimate and damaging to humanity.**

We are called, all of us,
**to raise our young with accurate and respectful information
about other traditions, religions, and cultures.**

We are called, all of us,
**to encourage positive appreciation of cultural and religious
diversity and to cultivate informed empathy with the suffering
of all beings.**

We are called, all of us,
**to show compassion to all,
even those we regard as enemies.**

We are so called,
and in the silence, we make our response… [Silence]

So may it be.

Gathering on the Third Compassion Sunday
Ordinary Time Year B

As spiritual people we have a responsibility
We are called to guard the role of compassion in our religious life.

The most important commandments which Jesus cited
focused on love of the sacred
and compassion towards humankind.

We are called to treat others as we would treat ourselves.
Who does not want to be treated with compassion?

Affirmation
(Said together as our offering prayer)

We affirm that compassion needs to be
a clear, luminous and dynamic force
in our polarized world.

We affirm that compassion is
rooted in a principled determination
to transcend selfishness.

We affirm that compassion can
break down political, dogmatic,
ideological and religious boundaries.

We affirm that compassion is
essential to human relationships
and to a fulfilled humanity.

We affirm that compassion is
indispensable to the creation of
a just economy and a peaceful global community.

We affirm that we seek to be people of compassion.

Gathering on the Fourth Compassion Sunday
Ordinary Time Year B

Compassion isn't just between you and me.
Compassion needs to spread throughout our nation.

Compassion needs to reach out around the world.
Compassion and kindness breed unity and peace.

Can we play the game with kindness and mercy?
Can we play the compassion card wherever we are?

Affirmation Of Faith said as an Offering Prayer
*(You are invited to join in with the affirmation,
saying as much as you can with integrity)*

Compassion calls us,
in both public and private life,
to refrain from causing consistent and emphatic pain
acting or speaking violently from spite, chauvinism, or self-interest,
impoverishing, exploiting, or denying basic rights to anybody,
inciting hatred by denigrating others
and denying our common humanity with even our enemies.

We acknowledge that we have failed to live compassionately
even, sometimes, in the name of religion.
We acknowledge our failures.

We re-commit to compassion,
to strong, firm loving and
to respecting all who share this earth with us.

Gathering for Wilderness Sunday, Creation Month
Creation Year B

All wild animals deserve care and attention
That includes the wild spirit within all of us.

Like the wolf befriended by St Francis,
our own inner, wild spirit needs befriending.
So we can grow in self-awareness, loving ourselves more completely.

Then we can be more aware of others
and love them as we love ourselves
May we have the courage to fully befriend ourselves and others.

Affirmation of Faith said as the Offering Prayer

We affirm the value of the wild in people and animals and plants.

**We affirm the importance of all having opportunity
to roam and grow and travel,
unhindered and unbound,
to feel wind rushing and water flowing
to feel the rising heartbeat
as difficult summits are scaled
and risky journeys undertaken.**

We affirm the need of the wildness within us
to have its freedom,
that we do not censor the creative impulse
or quash sudden intuition or divert unusual thought
only to be mannerly and polite.

**We affirm the risk inherent in following Jesus
on those wild journeys where he calls us onward,
where we may not find a place to lay our head
nor private nest or den for a hiding place.**

We affirm the need to befriend our inner wildness
so we can live and work and play with others
in harmony, not monologue,
in dialogue not monotone,
adding zest to our communal life,
each sparking life from the other.

**We affirm a person's right
to be individual, eccentric, or unusual,
and pursue their own path in life.**

We bring these offerings of food and money
to assist those
for whom living their own way in this world
brings shortages of different sorts
and to spread the good news
that everyone is loved and accepted just as they are.

*For a matching Blessing see the
Pairs of Responsive Gatherings and Blessings section.*

Gathering for a Service Where We Consider Power after a General Assembly

Power can be straight-line and mighty,
Obvious and overt.

Power can be less direct, even seem impotent,
but having an effect beyond its appearance.

Jesus chose the latter mode;
turning a cheek,
dying instead of conquering.
Which power will we exert?

Affirmation Of Faith

In a church
where power and domination 'over' seem to be winning
We affirm 'left-handed' power, the quiet and the creative.

In a church
where exclusivist, siege mentality seems to be dominant
We affirm the lifting of the drawbridge to invite others in.

In a church
which seems more like a club than a group of disciples
We affirm opening up the club to everyone.

In a church
where only some are brave enough to read and study and learn more
We affirm those who reach for learning and enlightenment.

In a church
which seems to want to define itself only in terms of heterosexuality
We affirm all orientations and genders are loved and included here.

In a church
which resists the Feminine and risks losing its soul
**We affirm that
all men and women are equally female and male
and we are all called to be whole as the divine is whole.**

Gathering Prayer for Wilderness Sunday
Creation 3 Year A

We give praise for the beauty of the earth
For this blue planet suspended in starry space

For the height and cragginess of mountains
For the smoothness of rolling foothills

For the silver sheen or rivers snaking their way to the sea,
For rolling surf and still lakes

For animals of every size and shape
For plants mysterious and bold

So much that nurtures our soul and feeds our bodies
Soothes our spirit and challenges our minds

We are in awe, words fail us
We fall into silent praise

[Silence]

Confession

We confess we have not always treated this earth
which has been gifted to us
like a home but rather like a rubbish dump.

We have not treasured the environment but plundered it
We have not cared where and how
the benefits of the earth come to us as long as they come.

We have not enquired whether the resources
we consume are renewable
or have been gained for us in ethical ways.

We have not known because we have not wanted to know
how much our consumption affects others
and the very earth itself, our life support system.

In the silence we ask forgiveness
for the ways in which we have knowingly,
and in ignorance, abused the creation.

[Silence]

Prayer for Ourselves and Others for Wilderness Sunday

We pray we may live together in Love and care for the earth
that as we pass through the wilderness experiences of our lives,
we may be alert to your Spirit's presence.

Guide the people of this land and all nations
in the ways of justice and peace
and of showing honour to the earth
so honouring each other and serving the common good
that we may preserve the wild places of our landscape
and care for the fragile and endangered
plants and animals which live in them.

May we all have a reverence for the earth as a precious creation,
that we may use its resources rightly in the service of others
May others see that we care for creation
and we care for people because they are precious human beings.

May all those whose lives are closely linked with ours be blessed
May we grant them the space to be
and enjoy the beauty of this world.

May we learn in the desert periods of our lives to love others better
May we walk alongside others
who suffer periods of doubt and despair.
As they walk in desert ways may we help them
In the desert periods of our lives
may we learn to love others better.

3 — Creeds

Creed for an Easter People

Death does not put a full stop on our experience
We live on in memory, through DNA, in artefacts we leave behind.
We live on through the influence we have had on others
– for good or ill.

Jesus lives on in us through
the influence of his teaching, wise and thoughtful
the caring behind his compassion, shown to many
the view he held of justice as the right of all.

We rejoice that therefore new life continually springs forth
phoenix-like from the ashes of life,
as seedlings flourish in the humus of the earth,
the old transformed within the grave of the chrysalis
into new forms previously unknown
which fill the world with beauty and delight.

Creed about Love

We believe all creation is good
that in each of us
is the divine spark of Love
and within us all are
a thousand possibilities and potentialities
for both good and evil.

We believe we are invited
to enter the ongoing struggle
of bringing to birth Love in our world
in more places and within more people,
of facilitating and celebrating
the deep union of sacred and secular.

We value Jesus who gives hope to ordinary people,
turning the regular into the special
showing the way of transformation
crashing through any boundaries
which separate us from Life.

We welcome the Spirit who can never be confined,
but appears in the most unexpected of places
always leading humankind
in the dance of life wherever it may lead.

Creed from South Canterbury, New Zealand

We believe in God, known to us in many ways.
By braided rivers threading through the rolling downs
in sunlit tussock on snow etched hills,
in small waves washing on the sweeping Bay.

We believe in Jesus known to us in many ways.
Through a life showing his love for all,
in parables that puzzle and challenge us,
in actions which make us gasp in pain and wonder

We believe in the Spirit known to us in mystery.
As daunting as the nor-west wind,
yet gentle as a candle flame,
breaking us open with warmth and energy.

We believe in the Church, this small vessel of fragile clay
into which are entrusted the many truths describing the divine
into which love is prodigally splashed without end
where we are baptised in trust and faith.

We believe that our belief is only true
when seen in action;
calming anxious minds
feeding fractured families
bringing faith in darkness.
Actions for which we depend upon grace
to call us, to empower and to guide.

4 — Affirmations

Affirmation for Advent Sunday
Advent 1 Year C

We trust that patient waiting
through times of gestation brings newness of life.
That the transformation of our lives
is made up of many small (and sometimes larger) advents,
periods of waiting followed by a birth,
our own lives becoming the 'rough stable'
in which Christ can be born again and again.

We have experienced that
many can then be attracted by that indefinable mystery
by the numinosity of the moment
by its irresistible appeal.

Captivated by pregnant promise,
by just a baby of an idea
or the childlike vulnerability of the moment
which reassures us we are understood
at the deepest depths of our being
– the depths where this new life gestates
and from where it is birthed.

We trust, we experience, but it is all still a mystery!

Affirmation for the Second Sunday in Advent

Advent 2 Year A

From our experience we affirm
that the divine energy we call God
frequently breaks through in unexpected places,
so small beginnings can have large consequences.

We affirm that listening is important
and it is alright to change your mind.

We affirm Joseph listening to his dream
and realising a just man can act justly in many ways.

We affirm divine presence is with us as it was with Mary and Joseph
when they stepped outside the norm and pushed boundaries.

We affirm virgin birthing is more than myth-as-fairytale,
but a living parable of spiritual renewal
which can be born in us, any day, any hour.

Affirmation of Prophets for the Third Sunday in Advent
Advent 3 Year C

We affirm the prophets
men like John the Baptist, women like Anna
who spoke out against injustice and greed,
calling the nation on its hypocrisy; foretelling a better future.

We affirm the word attributed to prophets like Zephaniah
and Mary in the Gospels,
stubbornly believing deliverance would come
that people now bound would be freed,
outcasts would be brought in
and those on the margin would become the centre.

In the light of their courage, we look within for strength
to be prophets in our own time,
speaking out about trade
which doesn't seem as fair as its title,
homes as scarce as ever,
poverty which does not seem to be
becoming history any time soon,
abuse and violence as rampant as ever,
diseases of our easy, civilized lives
which cripple bodies and minds.
Abuse of our planet which
leaves future generations in debt.

We affirm that we need help
from beyond ourselves
from amongst us and from within.

Affirmation and Recognition of Faith Found in Epiphany
Epiphany Year C

We recognise those moments of epiphany
– we've all had them –
when we have suddenly realised
everything has changed.
When we have seen deep down inside us
and found there what we did not expect.

Instead of the dark, greedy, grasping selfishness
we have been warned of all our lives,
we have discovered within, instead, light.
Light which children's drawings sketch around angels
light which softly glows with compassion and welcome,
beckoning us to own our inner rich resource
which is so like God
as to be no different from that we call divine.

We recognise, in those moments of discovery,
in those glimpses of the truth,
we can never be the same again,
even if the waters are deep and dark
we will be led through them
by a loving guide
who is, sometimes, us.

And thankfulness rises deep within.

Affirmation of Wilderness for the First Sunday in Lent
Lent 1 Year C

We affirm there is a journey to be followed
through the mazes of our lives,
a journey which can wind through wilderness
that lonely, awe-inspiring space
carved in solitude,
formed by silence.

We take heart that in wilderness
we inhabit a place Jesus walked before us.
That both wilderness and marketplace
are one in him,
and can be brought together in one unity
within us too, at the very deepest level.

We affirm that wilderness is
an integral part of a loving Creation,
that on desert paths we are accompanied by Christ
and when the Spirit's impetus
invites us to transformation within.

Affirmation Under a Fig Tree for the Third Sunday In Lent
Lent 3 Year C

We affirm that we do give a fig.
We give a fig about a lot of things:
Clean water for all,
Compassionate treatment of older people,
Security at the most mundane level,
Relief for cyclone and terrorism victims.

We think being spiritual is vital
for our lives to be in balance.
We know trusting the Way
even though where it will lead
may not be known,
keeps us open and vulnerable
in the best possible way.

We give a fig about peace
about justice, and about violence-free homes
and so today, as all days,
we vow to nurture fig trees in this orchard
so they will bear fruit
which nourishes humankind,
knowing the fruiting process
will be Spirit-led.

Affirming the Waste of Perfume on the Fifth Sunday of Lent
Lent 5 Year C

Like drops of perfume, our acts can be small
yet like its fragrance, fill the space around us.

We know even a small act different from expected practice
can expose us to ridicule and shame.

Yet, the fragrance of that offering can also linger
not only for that one night, but through centuries,
sweetening difficult dark moments for others,
far removed in time and space but not in circumstance,
the congruence of the moment creating a bond
with those who also wish to give what seems so little
and yet means so much.

We affirm small offerings.

We affirm brave movements made by frightened people
out of overpowering love.

We affirm courage in all its forms
and gratefully breathe in the fragrance of Love.

Affirmation of Faith for Easter

We believe in the One, who,
when there was nothing,
planted the seed of life in all creation,
green in the desert, blossom on the trees
and breath into the clay of human life.

We believe in Jesus,
eternal seed of life,
who entered the deaths of our existence,
trod deeply into our earthiness,
took into his body all our painfulness,
and lifted it into the victory of his love.

We believe in the Spirit
who waters our grief with tears,
nourishes in us the buds of life,
and tenderly cherishes our growings
until they break forth into the fruits of hope and faith.

We believe in the Church, a tree of life
grown from small beginnings
through generous acts of faith
sheltering under its branches those who come to it
continually refreshing itself through its roots
deep in the waters of life
which spring from the very heart of the divine.

An Easter Affirmation on Being Human
Easter 4 Year C

We affirm the beauty of being human
The tenderness of needing and thrill of desire.

We acknowledge the pain of being human
The agony of not getting and terror of the unknown.

We dare to trust that we are accepted and loved
In whatever way we respond to the challenges of life;
That there is a field of energy
in which we live and move and have our being
which upholds us
whoever we are, whatever we have done
wherever we are going or have been
whatever we believe or do not believe.

We do not have to be 'good enough'
to make this energy of love surround us,
it already does,
simply because we are human,
precious, honoured, and marvellous.

We affirm this to be true.

An Anzac Affirmation of the Work of Peacemaking
Easter 5 Year C
Sunday Anzac Commemoration

(Please join in where you can.)

We believe peace always must be fought for
though weapons of destruction may not be used in the cause
but rather weapons of love and forgiveness.

We believe peace always needs cherishing
for it can be easily lost when individual wants and desires
are rated more important than the common good.

We believe peace is hard to win
for it requires sacrifices of many kinds,
the putting of others before ourselves
or the putting of ourselves before others.

We believe there are many ways to achieve peace,
through doing, or through simply being.

We believe peace is not peace when it does not walk
hand in hand with justice, security, love and hope.

We believe peace between nations, or peoples,
between individuals and within families
springs from peace in each heart
and that peace in the heart springs
from the mysterious divine.

An Affirmation and Lament for Relationship on Trinity Sunday

Trinity Year C

We rejoice in moments when we 'click' with another
but lament when rapport with the other is absent.

We celebrate when family life 'works', bringing joy
but lament the occasions when it all falls apart.

We affirm the potential of structure and rules
but lament abuse of power which damages and limits human beings

We silently name those who brought and bring love into our lives…

[Silence]

And we lament times when love's only briefly felt or, worse, destroyed.
We silently seek healing from those moments in our lives…

[Silence]

We affirm the ability of the church to hold all securely
but lament how it can impede exchange of love between human beings

We affirm the beauty of the mysterious divine,
praying lamentation need not be everlasting
but that joy will come in the morning.

Affirmation of the Feminine
Mothers' Day Year B

We believe the feminine in our world is worthy of respect
not to be relegated to the dark shadows of consciousness
but brought into the open with dancing and with joy
recognising the integral role of the feminine in the divine.

We believe the creativity and birthing
traditionally associated as feminine
are vital to continuing health of body and soul,
not to be denigrated or devalued.

We celebrate that woman can be graceful and strong,
that she can lead and nurture
working with man as equal partner,
making this world a better place.

We celebrate the art of mothering
as it can be practised by male, female and transgendered
nurturing the young, protecting the vulnerable,
educating and forming mind and body.

We celebrate the art of homemaking
as it can be practised by females and males and transgendered
creators of comfort, gatherers, and providers of food,
cleaners and maintainers of safe spaces.

We rejoice in a world which is multigendered where we all can learn
to birth new life and mother it to maturity.

Where all can be like the divine, the Mother of all mothers.

Affirmation of the Word for Bible Month
Ordinary Time Year B

Events often have ineffable quality
impossible to capture in words.
Ancient women and men experienced more
than words on scroll or page ever detail.
So, we know scripture comes to us
filtered through minds and hearts,
contexts and circumstances.

In the events of our own lives
we can be moved by feather-light touches of grace
or tossed about in a maelstrom of meaning
or pain twists our gut in rictus agony.
So, we know divine words form in us
without sound or vocabulary,
shaped by who we are now.

Spoken or unspoken, the Word forms in us now
as formed long ago in people like us, yet not like us.
We sense its truth in feelings too deep for words
or thoughts too complicated for grammar.
So, we know the Word is all around us and within
In this, in all of us, is the Word of God.
Thanks be given.

A Wondering Affirmation

I wonder at the mystery we call God
Source of Life and Love,
Essence and origin of all creativity.
Mystery which wells up from within
and yet can be seen without and beyond;
silent as starlight,
sparkling as raindrops on spiders' webs,
silky, calm water reflecting the sky.

I follow the Way Jesus led women and men
when he lived on this earth;
A way of justice and compassion
of truth, integrity, and joy.
The way of love
expressed in his life as he became fully human
allowing us to glimpse how God might be.

I experience the Spirit of Love
breathing between and among humanity
a breeze which sets spring leaves trembling,
winds which roar across hill and harbour.
Spirit which empowers and animates
enabling us too to reach our fullest human potential.

I love the church when it encourages
women and men, young and old,
all colours of people, all orientations of relationships
to be fully human
and allow divinity to be seen in and through their lives.
I lament when church falls short of the goal
of loving, inclusive, human community
and limits the Love we call God.

Mystery, Way and Breath;
To wonder, follow and experience,
To become fully human in community,
This is our quest.

An Affirmation which Celebrates a Different Way
Ordinary Time Year B

We celebrate the tumbling of walls of prejudice and hate
and shattering of partisan treatment
towards those not 'in' the approved group
so enemies are loved and the unloved rewarded.

We celebrate moments when difference melts away
like a snowflake in sunlight;
When the just offers their umbrella
to the unjust as the rain falls upon them all.

We celebrate difference when it enriches our lives;
Bringing creativity where previously
there was beige or grey uniformity;
Exploding all the colours of the rainbow
over a black and white world.

We celebrate the courage
of those prepared to subvert the system
to defy orders to annihilate
to go to lengths to save another
by fulfilling inconvenient promises.

We celebrate the spirit
who moves in peoples' hearts,
encouraging the finding of another way,
supporting the alternative view,
orientating them towards justice,
so we may all be complete.

An Affirmation of Water at a Baptism
Ordinary Time Year C

We give thanks for living water poured out for us;
The splash of bathwater, cleansing and renewing,
transforming waters of baptism,
cool water gulped down on a thirsty day;

We give thanks for living water poured out for us;
Challenging words from long-ago prophets
healing words of an ancient psalm,
challenging words from the Teacher's heart;

We give thanks for living water poured out for us;
Loving words from the lips of loved ones,
praise from a demanding teacher,
inclusion by those with whom we want to be;

We give thanks for living water poured out for us;
Actions we did not expect on a day fraught and busy,
dreams in the night which illumine our days,
still small voice of God whispering in our hearts;

We give thanks for living water poured out for us.

Affirmation of Faith on the Fault line
Ordinary Time Year C

Living on the fault line of faith is uncomfortable;
Bedrock we thought was solid shows signs of slippage.
We wonder if the centre can indeed hold
And are nervous of the future.

Belief in propositions seems to be too unwieldly
for our fast-moving world;
As soon as we write them
they become inadequate in changing times.

Faith which is trust in the journey
proves more portable in our mobile world.
Faith which is relationship
provides companionship on the path.

We affirm the warmth of friendship,
We affirm the freedom of pilgrimage,
We affirm the value of doubt
and the appropriateness of uncertainty.

We affirm trust, hope and love
and the greatest of these is love.

Affirmation of Faithful Inclusion
Ordinary Time Year C
A caring community,
where everyone is valued and included regardless,
takes time and effort.

It requires paying attention
to those who may get lost among the crowd.

It requires compassion for those who struggle.
It needs grace for making space for those who are different.
It needs a lack of possessiveness or territoriality.
It depends upon dissolution of 'us and 'them' thinking.
It depends upon a firm centre with a permeable boundary
so anyone can enter and find their place
in relation to the centre which holds us all together.

We here today affirm our intention
to give that time, apply that effort, and seek that grace
so all truly feel welcome here.

Affirmation of Faith on an Anniversary

Ordinary Time Year C

We affirm the faith of those who have stood here
singing praise to the divine [for almost 140 years]
We affirm the faith of those who have knelt here
praying prayers of petition and praise.

We affirm the faith of those who preached here
reflecting on truths more ancient than time itself.
We follow those people of faith
differently in our time,
seeking to be honest
to developments of time and thought
yet also to be true to our soul's eternal cry
for peace and wholeness.

In our time and in our way,
we too, in these Gatherings accord worth
to all that is beautiful and lovely and true,
all that is honest and loving and just,
all that is far larger
and wider than our small concerns
yet which also intimately connects
with the yearnings of our hearts.

We, people of today's faith, we worship too,
calling worthy all that is good and true,
expressing the love that generates in our hearts.
We sing praise.

Affirmation of Compassion

Ordinary Time Year C

In our world there are those who have many resources
and those with few.
There are those who can offer comfort and support
and those who need it.
We all pass through stages
in which we may be the helper or may be needing help.
We move through life
from dependence to independence to inter-dependence.

We affirm our intention that
when we can, we will help in grace-filled ways,
when we need it, we will ask for grace to accept help offered.

We affirm our intention to show compassion with and for
all sorts and classes of people
young and old, the struggling and the successful
those in the centre and those at the margins.

We affirm all are loved, all are worthwhile, all are our kin.

Affirmation of Faith for a Learning Church
Ordinary Time Year C

Experience teaches ineffable lessons
hardly able to be expressed in words,
that which we 'know' without book learning or instruction.

Faith and trust grow as experience piles upon experience;
as soft as a feather's touch, as silent as a sunrise,
gentle as a kitten's paw, mysterious as a star lit sky
fearful, like blue-black thunderstorm, unsettling, like gale force wind.

Gently as mind is applied and thoughts of others scanned,
together we strain to express (with some sort of cognitive accuracy)
what it is we have come to know
by intuition and imagination, by myth and metaphor.

The task is not easy,
we do not always get it right,
but there is satisfaction in the wrestling,
growth in the struggle, even some serenity after striving.

And in the process, we find ourselves a little closer
to knowing the Ultimate and the Good.

Our intention?

To continue theologising
so faith reaches greater understanding.

Celebration of Faith

In this journey of life, we celebrate the divine map maker
Who creates roads twisting beyond our sight
Whose paths of light run across grassland and scree
Through tussock, over mountains;
Who has drawn in the sand a trail which never quite disappears;
We celebrate the One who calls pilgrims to the journey.

In this journey of life, we walk alongside Jesus our brother
Who gives us courage when the next turn reveals distant vistas;
Who is the light when our way lies through the dark night,
Who carries us when we cannot make our own footsteps,
We celebrate Jesus the brother-pilgrim.

In this journey of life, we celebrate the gifts of the Spirit;
Patience and self-control so we keep on journeying
Gentleness of those who deal kindly with our mistakes,
Faithfulness persisting when our blistered feet cry "no more!"
We celebrate the Spirit, sustainer of pilgrims.

In this journey of life, we celebrate our fellow travellers,
co-creators of the divine plan for our different pilgrimages
walking into the *missio dei* for the world.
Called by the divine, following the march of faith,
placing one step in front of the other in obedience and hope.
We celebrate the church on the move.

5 — Pairs of Responsive Gatherings and Blessings

Easter Day

Gathering

Easter Day Year C

Dawn has broken across a dark grieving world
New life is promised, with all the joy that brings.

Light is stealing across the landscape
Love begins to warm each heart.

The sweet-smelling fragrance of love is abroad
Alleluia! Alleluia!

Blessing

May the sweet-smelling fragrance of love
become part of the DNA of our lives
so, inevitably, it is carried from this place
to surround every person, every moment of every day.

A matching Creed is the first in the Creeds section.

Gathering

Easter Day Year B

From the noise and racket of Palm Sunday
Through the events of a tense and awkward Holy Week,

Into the twilight of Maundy Thursday
Through the darkness of Good Friday,

Into the silence of Easter Saturday
Then! New life bursts upon us this Easter Day,

From death to life,
We see and feel the grace of transformation,

Hallelujah!
Praise for this brand-new beginning!

Blessing

This Eastertide we embrace Life as shown to us that first Easter and lived out through centuries since.

We take with us this day the sure knowledge of Life within and Love surrounding us each moment of every day.

A Musical Service

Gathering

Music is a balm to the soul,
carrying messages we need, through melody and harmony.

Whether those messages be challenge, grief, joy, or praise,
music expresses deepest thoughts and yearnings.

Today we say 'thank you for the music'
as we look for the sacred within.

Blessing

The music of the spheres singing in our hearts,
We leave this place, to spread the music further abroad.

Music which soothes the sadness and comforts crying;
Music of life and love and laughter which lifts the spirit;

Music, sacred and divine,
which speaks to that which is sacred and divine within us all.

Gathering

Year A Pentecost 23

As followers of Jesus we seek to live
As he might have lived were he here.

What truths would he speak into our society?
What talk might he encourage?
What anger might he express?

How might we do all of those here and now in this place and time?
We seek wisdom and guidance
Wisdom and guidance greater than our own.

Blessing

Let us reach down deep
In order to stretch right up.

Let us think seriously
In order to live joyously.

Let us celebrate the breath of life within us
With plenty of oil to sing and dance by
so we can live in union deep within,
knowing Love surrounds us
every moment of every day.

> Used on the Sunday when the reading was from Matthew 25, the parable of the wise and foolish bridesmaids. See 'Now comes the bridegroom' in the hymn section.

Gathering

Ordinary Time Year B

What are we waiting for?
Are we ready for whatever will come, when it arrives?

Let us be present now, attentive and alert
Let us feel the consciousness arise with us.

Let us become more self-aware of how our lives are travelling
And how we are travelling within them.

Blessing

We recognise the need to engage
To not allow our intention to slide.

We go out in strength
To be as authentic as we can be through the power which is the Love that surrounds us every moment of every day.

Creation Month

Gathering For Planet Sunday

Creation 1 Year B

Planet earth is our home
And home to other creatures with us.

We live and breathe and sleep and work
here on this blue teardrop hanging in space.

We all need to breathe freely, live bravely and love deeply
We and all who share this home with us.

So may it be
Amen.

Blessing

We hold the line
Our planet's future hangs by a slender thread.

We hold the line
Our brothers the birds, our sisters the animals, need our help.

We hold the line
Because it makes a difference how we live in this home of ours.

We go out now, knowing that
Together we must be enough to love this world well enough.

We go out now, knowing that
Love surrounds us all every moment of every day.

After The Christchurch Massacre, March 2019

Gathering

Today we meet, shocked, enraged, saddened
that sisters and brothers worshipping together
were gunned down without mercy.

We seek the truth for today
so we can be one company of pilgrims together
in love and trust and solidarity of faith.

Blessing

We have watched and thought and prayed,
We have cried and yearn for our innocence back.

We go out now into a fractured world;
may we know how to be the glue which pieces us back together,
may we know how best to love and support those who are afraid,

making sure they know
Love surrounds us all every moment of every day.

6 — Prayers

Lord's Prayer

Planet spinning God, Pain bearing Christ, Energising Spirit
You are special beyond all knowing
We long for your commonwealth of peace
And truth to materialise
Here on this earth we inhabit.

We long for good to be achieved in our politics, society and families
We want each one on earth
To be well fed and clothed and housed every day.

We want the hurtful things we do to each other
To be healed, each showing the other forgiveness.

So those who war are reconciled
Relationships restored
And all united under the rainbow of your promise.

May we not be stretched beyond our limits
So evil overcomes our best intentions.

For yours is the rule of love
Whose power can transform the world
Now and forever. Amen.

Offering Prayer

Lent Year A

[Said together]

We are given many gifts,
among them is the created world of this planet,
which hangs like a blue teardrop in the inky blackness of space
Today in gratitude we bring back something of that gift;
some money for this church's work here and beyond these walls
and some food for those who have little.

We bring also ourselves as grateful beings,
ready to do our part to save this planet
so its waters may always be blue and pure,
its forests green and lush and its creatures safe and 'here'.
May all our gifts be blessed and fruitful,
Amen

Prayer of Adoration and Confession

This [World Communion] Sunday we give thanks for our world
For our beautiful blue planet hanging in space

For all the waters of the earth, the seas and lakes and rivers
For all the animals, big ones and small ones

For the people who inhabit the globe
For children of every colour and hue

For nations and tribes, clans and communities
For the kinship we feel today with the millions of others

Who are brothers and sisters with us in the faith
Worshipping like us this day as earth turns further into light.

If we have done wrong to other people whether they be like us or different
We ask forgiveness.

If another person has hurt us
In the silence we ask forgiveness

[Silence]

7 — Lament and Litany

Thanksgiving and Lament
Advent 2 Year A

We give thanks for the new life children bring to their worlds
**We give thanks for all villages of the world
who have raised children in their midst.**

We give thanks for communities where
Mary, Jesus and Joseph lived.
We give thanks for those, like them,
who courageously take risks so children will survive.
For this we give thanks.

We lament that not all children are welcome in the world
and solo mothers are often rejected and poorly treated still.

We lament that because of prejudice,
people are afraid to step out and do the unusual,
to push boundaries, or stand up and be counted.

We lament limiting theology which may arise
in some places from this reading of the Word;

We lament those times when for different reasons
people have not listened to or acted on their dreams.

This is our lament.

Litany of Thanksgiving

For the everlasting sacred,
like eternal snows feeding great glaciers
We give thanks and praise for eternal love.

For the sacred majesty of peaks,
rising high above foothills, valleys, and plains
We praise benign and compassionate rule.

For divine beauty,
like misty blue foothills between mountain and plain
We express today pleasure and delight.

For the sacrificial love of the man Jesus
whose cross stands tall on spire and hill
We give thanks for persistence and integrity to the end

For the risen One
striding these hills with us on daily pilgrimage
We give thanks for his brotherhood and companionship.

For the vitality of divine vision waving over us like
undulating tussock over golden foothills
We give thanks for inspiration and the Call to move on.

For the winds of the Spirit
blowing from nor'west, the east and the south
We give thanks for freshness and renewal come upon us.

For the blessing of the Spirit
weaving her way through lupin and beech, over pasture and riverbed
We give thanks for new growth and grounding in earth.

For the rush of the Spirit flowing in full flood,
tumbling over rock and stone, twisting in gentle braids,
**We give thanks for blessing, which is life giving, refreshing,
beautiful and free.**

For goodwill of people braiding lives together
We give thanks for willingness to gather and join.

For faith woven into this landscape over time
**We give thanks for faithfulness and loyalty,
for being braided together by more than geography,**

Tumbled and tossed by divine power and energy
divinely abraded and smoothed, eroded and carved;
**for being made living stones fit to be one people,
we give praise God, Son and Spirit.**

Indeed, we give praise for the divinity
in whom we live and move and have our being
In which we know loving and giving, blessing and embracing
from alpine slope to sea's shore, from river to strait,
from coast to coast;
**in whom we know the height and depth,
the length and breadth of Love.**

Thanks be given, **Amen.**

8 — Communion Liturgies

Great Prayer of Thanksgiving for the Season of Creation

The Spirit be with you
And also with you.

Lift up your hearts.
We lift them up.

Let us give thanks.
It is right to offer thanks and praise.

It is indeed right to give thanks,
With the whole created universe
We praise the unfailing gift of life
We give thanks that we have been made human.

Love came among us in Jesus Christ,
Who makes all things new, not only renewing us,
But bringing the promise of a renewed creation,
A new heaven and a new earth,
With reconciliation of all peoples.

Therefore, with those who have walked this earth before us
Whether by belief or by other paths,
with all those who share this planet with us now
Its vast oceans and tall mountains, its serene lakes, and flowing rivers,
Stormy moments and myriad creatures, joyfully we say:
Holy, holy, holy, Love, Life, and Energy
Earth and sea and sky and all that lives
Declare your presence and your glory.

Jesus, our brother,
Made known to us afresh each time in the breaking of bread;
Who, on the night he was handed over to be killed,
When he was with his friends, much like us,
Took bread, gave thanks, broke it and said:
'This is my body which is for you
Do this to remember me.'

In the same way also the cup after supper saying
'This cup is the new covenant in my blood.
Do this whenever you drink it, to remember me.'

Great Prayer of Thanksgiving for Peace and Justice
Peace be with you.
And also with you

Lift up your hearts.
We lift them up.

Let us give thanks.
It is right to give thanks and praise

It is indeed right to offer thanks and praise
For to our troubled earth came Jesus the man
Who walked with people rather like us
And talked of peace with justice for all
**Who set before us a way of living that valued all people and
Called for respect to be paid to the lowest of the low;
Who kept to his principles despite opposition and betrayal.**

And here in this favoured land,
Non-aligned and relatively uninvolved in present conflict
We hear his message of grace for all, of love to each person
And of the chance to begin again where we have failed
Because of his resistance to evil
In the battle for the commonwealth of God
**As he asked us, we follow his example of making real peace
Ensuring justice is done and people freed from oppression.**

So, with the women and men for whom he fought against ignorance
And with the men and women who have worked for peace
Both within and without the church through the ages
And with those who stand for peace now
Carrying his cross in their time, we sing:

**Holy, holy, holy One
Source of power and might
Heaven and earth are full of your glory
Hosanna in the highest.**

Blessed be our brother Jesus,
Bone of our bone and flesh of our flesh
From whom the cup of suffering did not pass
But whom on the night on which he was betrayed
While he was eating the Passover with his friends
People much like us,
 took bread, gave thanks, broke it, and said:

**'This is my body which is for you
Do this to remember me.'**

In the same way also the cup after supper saying
**'This cup is the new covenant in my blood
Do this whenever you drink it, to remember me.'**

Therefore, we eat this bread and drink this cup
We proclaim grace and peace till the end:
**Come now, disturbing spirit
Breathe on this bread, risen in the warm
And this wine crushed in its bitter sweetness
So that all we take in is transformed into new possibilities
And all we offer is available for the transformation of the world.**

Communion Liturgy from the South Pacific

Grace and peace be with you.
And also with you.

Lift up your hearts.
We lift them up.

Let us give thanks.
It is right to give thanks and praise.

It is indeed right to give thanks for,
This long of long white cloud with mountain spine
Coastal seas and tussock hills, chequered plains, and tranquil lakes
And the birth of Jesus of Nazareth
in another land, brown, where this is green, dry, where this is lush
The companion with us always
Even in this southern set of isles
Under this southern sky.

With the whole created universe
With the birds and animals of this land
Sea lion, seal and penguin,
Albatross, tui and pukeko,
We praise you for your unfailing gift of life.

Therefore, with south pacific saints and southern prophets
And all the redeemed in this far-flung land and beyond
who forever sing to this glory, we say:
Holy, holy, holy
Source of power and might
Heaven and earth are full of glory
Blessed is he who comes in the name of the divine.

Blessed is our brother Jesus
bone of our bone and flesh of our flesh
From whom the cup of suffering did not pass
But whom on the night on which he was betrayed
While he was eating the Passover with his friends
People much like us,
took bread, gave thanks, broke it, and said:
'This is my body which is for you
Do this to remember me.'

In the same way also the cup after supper saying
'This cup is the new covenant in my blood
Do this whenever you drink it, to remember me.'

Therefore, we eat this bread and drink this cup
We proclaim grace and peace till the end:
Come now, disturbing spirit
Breathe on this bread, risen in the warm
And this wine crushed in its bitter sweetness
So that all we take in is transformed into new possibilities
And all we offer is available for the transformation of the world.

Great Thanksgiving for World Communion Sunday

Peace be with you.
And also with you.

Lift up your hearts.
We lift them up.

Let us offer thanks and praise.
It is right to offer thanks and praise with grateful hearts.

It is indeed right for Love does not lord it over us
But walks on our earth in one human being and in all humankind,
All over the earth of this planet,
Lovingly open to every woman, man
And non-binary person of every race or creed

We seek help in walking as freely on the earth as Jesus did
Seeking the same determination and courage
To face obstacles to justice and peace in our own world,
In our own time.

Seeking to walk the Way in a manner worthy,
Not only of our companion Christ,
But worthy also of those who share this planet with us
In grateful spirit for the diversity of humanity
And for all who worship in the Spirit
On the plains of Africa, beside the rivers of India,
On the steppes of Russia, in North American skyscrapers,
In the Australian outback and South American rainforest
On the mountains of Europe, in crowded Asian cities,
on Pacific atolls and through this land of beauty, Aotearoa.

Offering thanks and praise for Love
For the Spirit's continuing presence with us
We join with them saying...

Holy, holy, holy Love
Whose power is greater than might,
All this world sings of your beauty,
Blessed are they who spread this word abroad.

9 — Responsive Blessings

Blessing on Matariki
Matariki Year A

Mostly, everyone needs a new start,
a beginning which acknowledges the past
with all its triumphs and mistakes

but which allows us to move forward
vowing to do better with our own and others' lives.

Matariki gives that new start today.
Let us go beyond these walls
and let those we live and work and play with
know that Love surrounds us all every moment of every day.

Blessing for Wilderness Sunday
Creation 3 Year A

May we have learned
never to tame the wild impulse of Love
demonstrated to us in Jesus' life, work and death.

As we go from here let us encourage
the organic, flowing wildness of Love
as we see it flowing forth into the world from this community
and from the community of all the Wild Ones on this planet.

So may it be.

Blessing for Those Who Journey
Epiphany Year C

Others on the spiritual path believed differently in other times.
Our task is to learn what we can trust
as our source, direction, and goal now,
sharing with others what may be helpful for them.

Blessed be all who journey,
all who seek, all who question.
**May all find that
Love surrounds us every moment of every day.**

Blessing for the Third Sunday in Advent
Advent 3 Year C

For those who have no joy in their hearts,
For those whose lives are full of difficulty,

For those who are anxious and have no peace,
We have lit the candle of joy.
We go out remembering the call to be bearers of joy in a troubled world.

Blessing for the Fourth Sunday in Advent
Advent 4 Year C

For those who look for love, but are abused,
For those who have lost family and friends,

For those who live where there is strife or war,
We have lit the candle of love.
We go out now to serve Love in the world.

10 — Poems

Advent

The Door

Christmas Eve Year B

I have seen many doors.
Some are homely
and open eagerly with a warm invitation to "Enter, do!"

Others, glass with advertising etched upon them,
slide open noiselessly
inviting me into the mall to spend my money,
as much as possible, please.

There's the door to work where I enter
some mornings, gladly, or not so.
Other doors, ecclesiastical grey,
have been firmly padlocked for years.

This door lies ajar, a glimpse beyond of simplicity and rustic charm
over laden with mystery and awe, mother's milk and animal aroma.

It is not a world I know well,
twenty first century urbanite that I am these days.
If I enter this world, will I know what to do? Will I be welcome?

Do I have the key which unlocks this world
interpreting its symbols and its mystery
so I know what I need to know?

The door is ajar,
One simple movement from me and it will swing wide
wide enough for everyone to enter.
Crossing the threshold seems an exceedingly small step
yet one as wide as a universe
and as deep as an ocean.

Will I take that step?
Or always be left wondering what might have been?

Midnight

Christmas Eve Year C

The deepest, darkest time
Midnight,
Mid way through the night of dark and sorrow
Right in the middle of the feeling of abandonment
Free to fill the mind with anxiety and fear
When other voices fall asleep

Are we being told there is light which can shine
even in our darkness?
One which will not abandon us
even when all others fall asleep?

Midnight split in two
Once only dark
Now light, glorious light
Seeps through the clenched fingers
Beats gentle on closed eyelids
Hugs tired shoulders
And lifts the drooping arms
So we can see the dawn
Which is even now breaking
Across our tear-blurred sight.

Silently, in the middle of the night,
The new day we did not dare to hope for
Begins as the light comes into the darkness
Which cannot put it out.

Christmas

Morning After the Night Before
Christmas Day Year C

When you awoke,
Tired, bruised
Did you wonder if you had dreamed it?
When you saw the sheepskin
Did you then believe the visit
From those inarticulate and smelly shepherds
Had really happened?

Then hidden underneath the skin,
The gold, where Joseph had tucked it for safety,
And the incense, (strange gift for a child),
And did your brow furrow further
As you saw the myrrh alongside?
Their words now suddenly clear in your mind,
The solemnity, the warning…

Then, abruptly, you are full awake and packing,
Getting ready to begin this lifetime
Of being mother,
The mother of a little boy baby
Whose life would change the world
Even more than he had just changed yours.

Lent

Brought to Tears

Lent 2 Year C

The journey to Jerusalem is never easy,
not any easier now,
with this dread feeling
that it was all for the last time.
Those moments when it seemed
you walked in slow motion,
all sound muted;
looking at and seeing the faces,
but not hearing their words
your own mind racing

"Listen!" you wanted to shout, "Listen now!
Take heed of what I say! Now! I won't be back, you know!"

When you saw the city
the beloved temple gleaming in the setting sun
suddenly it was all too much, and the tears came.

So many times, Jerusalem had been told the good news.
So many times, it had not listened,
its sophisticated multicultural society
believing it was too knowledgeable to need to look inside
and see what was needed – what was the 'one thing necessary'.

It was too much to bear without tears filling your eyes,
dropping one by one on the dusty path
one by one down the steep hillside,
bouncing off shiny olive leaves,
hissing into steam on sun scorched ground.
Tears of frustration and grief, tears of love.

There's not much beautiful about being broken

Written after seeing the wreckage of churches in Christchurch after the earthquakes of 2011.

Could be used as a reflection at Easter or during Lent.

It may also fit Reformer's Sunday.

There's not much beautiful about being broken
Prosaic cyclone fencing saves passers by from further injury
But today no sunlight glints on raindrops
To encrust them with diamonds
No aesthetic design lines lift the spirit

The footing of a mighty church laid low is no inspiration
Only commemoration of glories once-been
Piles of rubble beg the question
Of whether these stones will ever
Sing out to us again of transcendence and divinity

Spires and steeples are no longer
reliable signposts to where we thought God lived
The mighty spire which told us God was up there
is now down here among us.

Is God here too?
Where is God now
when church doors are closed on broken masonry shells,
'Danger' written in red?

'Church after church' they are saying now
'has been disproportionately hit by these tremors of the earth.'
In proportion though to the degree to which the church has
(or more frequently) has not updated itself.

The inertia of establishment preventing renewal
symbolised by the vulnerability of its buildings to seismic shock
imitating the inertia of complacent belief
that eternal verities need no renewal
or adjustment to changing contexts
so we could fool ourselves we still had the answers
not realising the questions had changed.

By all means let us mourn
the passing of beloved windows memorialising our dead
organs which may sing no more
sanctuaries safe no longer
but let us also mourn our own rigidity
our unreadiness to be renewed
which these new fault lines have exposed;
Our own faulty assumptions
that 'eternal' meant' unchanging'

Let us weep
Let us wail and gnash our teeth
not over tumbled bricks
but the hardness of heart which has left us prone.

And when we have cried each tear to the very last
then let us reconsider
how we will be church again
Will we resist this seismic shock
learn no lessons,
build again with little change?

Or, will we hear the message in the creaking of the earth
read the signs in the tearing open
(with the same conviction of the Calvary moment)
of our holies of holies?

And will we ask the right questions:

'what has this crucifixion come to save us from?'
and
'what shape can resurrection take this time?'

Christchurch, New Zealand, 8 August 2011

Easter

Unseasonable journey

I remember it as if it were yesterday
the day he set his face
and turned towards Jerusalem.

We all knew that look,
all of us women
who followed him
Mary, Joanna,
Susanna and the rest,
we knew, all of us,
once that look was in his eyes
and his jaw set in that determined way
nothing any of us could say could change his mind.

An autumn chill
whispered its way
around my heart
the long, lovely summer
of camaraderie and companionship
was over

for I knew
we all knew
(especially him, although he never said)
death
lay at the end of this unseasonable journey

Looking back now,
I remember the slow,
inevitable
irrevocable
feel of that time

his words falling on our ears
as leaves fall
one by one
from trees
weeping away their life
in golden tears

afterwards, we looked back,
surprised at the depth
of golden leaves
which had gathered at our feet

the first few leaves
fluttered gently to the ground
as he told the men to let the children be
'the kingdom belongs to such as these,' he said.
We women knew what he meant
we know children
the gut honesty
that hasn't been veneered with social graces yet.
We knew what he meant.

And it seemed a single golden leaf
gently touched my hair
As I heard him say
'Mary has chosen the better part
it shall not be taken from her'

and it hasn't.

A few more leaves fell
when he wept over the city

the stormy tension was all through Jerusalem
like one of those autumn storms
that pulls leaves from the trees in jealous fury

but once,
there was a lull,
when, through the heavy scent of ointment
above the woman's tears he said to the stony faces
above him
'she has done this for my burial'
and a shower of golden leaves
joined the others on the ground.

But autumn ends
with gaunt skeletons
against a wintry sky

and so his end came
on a gaunt tree
starkly black
amidst a darkened day
and a chill of winter
settled on my soul
the pile of leaves
about my feet
lost their glow
as the promises lost their power.

The cold went deep within me,
and even when love had burst forth
out of season
life in the middle of death
warmth in the heart of winter,
and the leaves at my feet
had regained their golden glow
for now I knew the promises were true
the memory of that desolation remained

Reminding me God does not wait for spring
but offers life in winter
for love knows no season.

Luke 8:2-3 & Luke 9:51

Today

Easter Day Year A

Today,
we Christians
(yes, us, that stuffy lot)
are making the country happy
(well, perhaps not retailers in tourist towns)
but definitely
we are making others happy today.

They get to have a holiday on this holy day
accompanied by chocolate eggs
and other forms of chocolate which have
been woven into the urban legend over the years.
(This year I saw a chocolate kiwi in the supermarket aisles.)

It's right the general population
is invited
to enjoy, to re-create, to celebrate
at Easter
for that is what we celebrate too
the joy,
the release,
the freedom,
(chocolate covered or not.)

Today we embrace the Spirituality of Life,
Thankful we have come through the darkness of death.
We are more than only unscathed.
Easter reminds us
there is transforming power afoot in the world
and, if we allow it,
it might just transform us!

Pentecost

Spirit Wind

"God is more than two men and a bird"[4]

A bird?
Birds, chicks,
Why do women get to be delicate, feathered creatures,
while men are lions, bulls, tigers?

In the language of sacred scripture
you, spirit, are wind – *ruach*.
Ruach, in Hebrew,
a feminine zephyr.

The Greeks called you *pneuma*,
a neutral term,
and we choose not to call you 'it,'
so why do we not call you 'she,'
give you the gender you deserve
related as you are
to another sister
wise *Sophia*?

But you, Spirit,
you come as *ruach*
blowing through our lives.
You are the Life Giver.

Who could you be but Woman?

---

[4] Sandra M. Schneiders, "Women in the Fourth Gospel and the Role of Women in the Contemporary Church" BTB 12 (1982):35-45.

Aotearoa Pentecost

Pentecost is here!
In this New Zealand autumn,
leaves of blazing colour
fall upon me,
blown down from above
by rushing wind.

Leaf shapes, flame shapes
shaped like tongues,
yes,
tongues of fire.

They nestle on the earth
so I know in the midst even of winter
there is life;
that I need not
be locked away in dead wood
and bare branches
but can be alive and free
for it is Pentecost
and the Spirit has come!

Come with flame
and wind
and excitement, hope and joy!

Cartwheel across the lawn!
Run through the piles of leaves!
Run with the wind in your face and at your back!
Smile until your face can stretch no more!

The Spirit has come
for Real!

It is here!

A 'Silent' Pentecost

A poem written during a silent retreat

Walking seawards, I find celebration there.
Praise crashing on the shore,
the roar of joy in my ears.
Spume blowing off the curling wave,
splashes in delight,
a foaming cascade on the beach.

Silent?

Pentecost silent?

Walking homeward,
warm nor-wester blows in my face,
I sing into the wind.
Divine breath,
rushing wind,
you are so strong
but gentle.

A lively silent Pentecost.

And look, up there,
light streams through massing clouds
and falls on mown hay,
on mountains white with early snow,
on autumn leaves,
bright tongues of fire still clinging to the trees.

The Spirit is here,
in mighty breakers,
in northwest wind,
in every changing light,
and leaves of fire.

The Spirit is all around me,
and within.

11 — Reflections from a New Perspective

Truth and Factuality: Babies and Stardust
– a Reflection for Christmas Day on Luke 2

Doesn't everyone know the story? Is this Christmas story which we celebrate in carol and children's story true or fact? The two are not necessarily the same, Fred Dagg for New Zealanders is a truly real character, yet he is the figment of the comedian John Clarke's humorous imagination.

Wal and Cooch of Footrot Flats tell us a true story about us as a nation, especially about the men of our nation and yet they are fictional cartoon characters.

The angels whom we will sing about at the end of today's service tell us a truth whether or not even in these times of quantum physics, angels may still be yet more elusive than the Higgs boson.

In ancient scriptures, not only Christian ones, angels play the role of messengers of the supreme symbol of God. Mostly, in the scriptures, whenever a human being has an especially spiritual moment, a God-like 'aha', an angel is somewhere in the story, Hagar met an angel in the desert, Jacob wrestled with one in the darkness, Elijah was fed by them when he was feeling most down, Jesus was helped by them when he was tempted. When humans are most down on their luck, most rejected, more outcast, God, symbolised by angels and sometimes represented by dreams, enters the scene.

So when the Gospel writers, other than John, include angels in the story, they are telling us this story has God dimensions, that it is as big as God can ever be. That here is an intersection between the divine and the human. Angels are like a great big signpost or set of advertising hoardings saying, "Watch the man this child will grow into! Listen to what he says! Follow him! This is news which will bring you great joy and all the world with it if we follow him in his quest." So might the writer or writers of the Gospels speak to us today, staggered that we might miss the point because we might be arguing over factuality versus truth.

Don't let your search for factuality blind you to the truth of this amazing story. The baby is real, he is a factuality; the stardust scatted over this story through the centuries may not be as factual, yet truth lurks within the story, is seen in these characters, and brings light into our various types and kinds of darkness. Whatever our particular kind of corner which needs illuminating and however dark it can sometimes get, it cannot quench the light of love.

The Storm on the Lake – Mark 4:35-41

We develop through our lives. Like fishers who fished the Sea of Galilee learned their profession. We get skilled knowing how to mend a net well, developing callouses hauling nets, honing instincts about wind and weather, water and wayfinding, barely noticing the rocking of the boat, easily balancing ourselves between peaks and troughs of fortune. As we grow older, these skills accumulate. Nothing can throw us, at least, not daily.

Then, one day, everything changes. The storm we had sensed was brewing is bigger and more ferocious than every other storm thus far in our life. It rocks our little boat severely. We are mortally afraid our life will totally capsize.

The usual tricks don't work – denial, obfuscation, pretence that all is well, baling out furiously – the storm still rages. Depression wraps the brain in cotton wool. Relationships break up. Careers founder and fail. What has been satisfying becomes dull and boring. The joy goes out of life. The danger of being swamped by it all, is real.

We look around for another remedy; one we haven't tried before. We find we need, in a metaphorical sense, to wake up. To become more conscious. To truly grasp the significance of this challenge. This is no time for our deeper Self to be snoozing away at the heart of our craft. We can't sort this while we remain unconscious.

The storm continues… Desperately shaking the sleeping shoulder, we discover with a shock that the teacher of wisdom we need is our own Self. We have woken up Wisdom lying within. The effect is uncanny.

While the practicalities of the moment take a little longer to sort, in the moment we surrender to that inner wise voice, we access stillness. We are in the eye of the storm.

Serenity floods the soul, not the raging waters. Now we are wide awake to the inner resources there in our little boat all the time. Peace replaces panic. We may encounter rough seas again, but no storm will threaten our very fabric as much ever again.

Different kinds of waste – Luke 15:11-32

You can only do it when you are young, gather up hard won resources which are barely yours and scatter them about. Using them to win favour and curry friendship with others like you who only have the short term in focus. It is all high day and holiday for a while and when you can remember the night before, you remember it as fun and games.

It's such a good time you do not notice the falling bank balance, the less than healthy lifestyle and the jading of the palate.

Afterwards you wonder if you could have survived if the crash hadn't come, but, newly honest with yourself, you knew you had brought your ruin on yourself. You had not only lost friends and money and health, but you had also lost yourself in the frenetic auctioning of resources.

As you sit in the piggy mess of your broken world, you wonder who you are anymore. To whom do you belong – to anyone at all? Or are you alone in this harsher world not insulated with money and beauty and talent?

You think back to a wiser person you once thought controlling and demanding, but who, you feel even in this crisis of your own making, would at least be fair. Who might take you in, provide some minimal shelter, work, hopefully congenial, even if hard?

So, you make the walk of shame. Long days, dusty landscapes as you reflect on what has been, on what might have been and now, what on earth can be.

Practising your abject speech, head down, you enter the space inhabited by those who knew you growing up, who know your genealogy, your former place in the world. You know the reaction to those who waste inheritances is not good and you brace yourself for the first stone, for the spittle, another projectile which will unerringly find its way to your cheek.

No spitting. No stone has anytime to land, for a rough and warm embrace shields you from the assault you deserve. Panting at the unaccustomed exercise, the wise one, though wounded by you, now welcomes you with a flurry of robes and a flurry of words and orders barked abroad. " This is my child! Lost! Now found! Ring! Robe! Fatted calf!"

You knew there was a journey, but you thought that was for others now you had shamed yourself. But in this moment, you know, there is a journey you can walk, and you are on it, have always been on it and always will.

You were the one who stayed at home. Life had been tough. Twice the work, half the resources, half the fun too; that youngest sibling had brought joy and laughter though you would have been the last to admit it.

You came to resent the constant demand of the work

You were grumpy and surly, and the easy friendship with you and your parent had fallen away. Though from that side one always felt calm, rocklike acceptance. Despite the shame of being thought of as those who had been duped. Despite the sense of rejection felt just as keenly by both of you.

Just when you thought it couldn't get worse, the whippersnapper came home. Tail between the legs only for a moment. For parental welcomes flowed generously, foolishly, wastefully. After all your sacrifice, it was too much!

Even the quiet conversation in the field did not fix it. The problem your own stubbornness. (Just like your sibling's if you had been aware enough to see it). Blocking the flow of love, wasting the moment like wasted money.

Wasted opportunity, trapping the psyche in the darkness, shrivelling the soul.

Shame.

Recent & forthcoming books by Susan Jones from Philip Garside Publishing Ltd

Wherever You Are, You Are On The Journey:
Conversations in a Coffee Shop Book 1

Do you feel there is more to Christian faith than is told on Sundays? Are you questioning whether the firmly held beliefs you grew up with are going to be useful in the next stage of your life?

Don't panic! You have simply reached a transition point in your faith journey.

Hope and her minister/mentor Susan chat about deepening & re-enchanting faith at their local café.

(Print and eBooks now available.)

We are All Equally Human:
Conversations in a Coffee Shop Book 2

Charity, a young lesbian church goer, attends her church's national conference, and finds herself hurt and upset by the swirl of the 'gay debate' in the Church. She comes home puzzled and worried.

Charity and her minister plunge into coffee shop conversations about this issue.

(Print and eBooks publishing in 2022.)

Being Woman in the World:
Conversations in a Coffee Shop Book 3

Faith's weekly coffee bar conversations with her minister explore the Feminine – in psychology and theology, women in biblical texts, roles in church and society, God and gender, women and spirituality. They cover the range!

(Print and eBooks publishing in 2022.)

CPSIA information can be obtained
at www.ICGtesting.com
Printed in the USA
LVHW050819090322
712947LV00015B/405